The Lean Marketplace

Edited by Ville Saarinen
Design by Janne Koivistoinen
Produced by Sjoerd Handgraaf

Imprint: Sharetribe

ISBN: 978-952-94-0008-9

If you'd like to read more about online marketplaces, check out the Marketplace Academy at www.sharetribe.com/academy. We regularly publish articles about running a marketplace business, growth and marketing, as well as inspiring interviews with other marketplace entrepreneurs.

Acclaim for
The Lean Marketplace

"Juho and Cristóbal have written a practical in-the-weeds guide on marketplace execution that will prove invaluable for all entrepreneurs looking to start a marketplace. No fluff, just actionable ideas."

– **Sangeet Paul Choudary,** best-selling author of Platform Revolution and Platform Scale

"Building marketplaces can be hard. The Lean Marketplace is a very useful step-by-step guide to help entrepreneurs think through the challenges and solutions to create the next Uber or Airbnb."

– **Boris Wertz,** Founder and General Partner, Version One Ventures

"Must read for every marketplace entrepreneur. I'm going to ask everyone in our our team to read this book."

– **Bram de Zwart**, Co-founder and CEO, 3D Hubs

"As I'm friends with both authors, I know first hand that the information in their book is hard won from long experience helping dozens of marketplaces succeed and consulting the top experts from around the world. However, the quality and comprehensiveness of the content speaks for itself. It covers all the essentials of growing an online marketplace, and in the most straightforward way possible. It is an impressively practical, must read resource for any current or aspiring marketplace entrepreneur. I can't recommend it highly enough, but please see for yourself."

– **Neal Gorenflo**, Co-founder of Shareable

"The essential guide to building an essential marketplace."
– **Tristan Pollock**, Co-founder, Storefront, Partner, 500 Startups

"Reading Juho's and Cristobal's advice online before launching our platform helped us save so much time and avoid the most common mistakes. If you're considering building a marketplace business, read this book first. Seriously."
– **Agne Milukaite**, Co-founder and CEO, Cycle.land

"Envisioning, validating, building and growing a marketplace is no small challenge: the most important aspect to nailing this challenge down is all about avoiding losing time and energy in the myriad of wrong directions that can come up your way. This book is an essential guide, the lifeboat for the marketplace founder that faces the ocean of bootstrapping."
– **Simone Cicero**, platform strategist and consultant, creator of Platform Design Toolkit

"I bootstrapped my marketplace business from launch to profitability in 6 months. Reading this book will help you do the same."
– **Mike Williams**, CEO and Founder, Studiotime

Table of contents

Introduction

In May 2015, we had a discussion about our experiences in helping marketplace entrepreneurs with their fledgling businesses. We noticed that both of us had heard the same story multiple times: an enthusiastic small team has a big vision of how their marketplace will change the world. They start building their business. Soon, the struggle begins. What seemed easy on paper turns out to be extremely challenging in practice.

Make no mistake: not all marketplace ideas are great. Some of them deserve to die. However, most marketplace businesses that fail today don't fail because the idea itself is bad—they fail because of poor execution. People keep making the same mistakes over and over again. If only people were aware of these situations and knew how to handle them, mistakes could be avoided.

We were both fans of the Lean Startup approach to validating business concepts quickly and with as little waste as possible. However, we realized that the existing books about the topic were lacking a practical approach for applying the method to building a two-sided marketplace in particular. Marketplaces are quite specific in nature, and building them requires specific knowledge. Previously, this knowledge has been acquired mostly through trial and error; only once you've built a marketplace business or two do you become an expert on these topics. That's how we learned this stuff over the past 10 years: by banging our heads against the wall ourselves, and watching countless other people do so as well.

It doesn't have to be this way. There's no need to learn everything the hard way. The applicable tactics and techniques can be studied in advance, helping you avoid the most common pitfalls.

This is what this book is about. It's a handbook for anyone building an online marketplace. The same methods will apply whether your organization is a startup, a cooperative, a non-profit, or a big brand. Not every marketplace will be as big as Airbnb and Uber, but we believe there are thousands of marketplace ideas out there that can make for great, sustainable businesses. With the help of this book, you're one step closer to building the next one.

February 2018, in Helsinki and Barcelona,
Juho Makkonen and Cristóbal Gracia

1

What you need to know before starting your marketplace business

_____

Online marketplaces are hot. The success of platforms like Airbnb, Etsy and Uber has proven that the marketplace model is very scalable and can be applied to pretty much any area of business. As one of the top VC firms, Andreessen Horowitz, put it: "This is just the beginning."[1]

There's no better time to become a marketplace entrepreneur. In the coming years, we're going to see tremendous innovation in the field of building and running marketplaces.

However, even though the time is right—and the technology is finally mature enough—building a successful marketplace is far from a trivial task.

Before we start, a word of warning: there are no shortcuts to launching a marketplace and making it successful. Having a sound strategy and knowing the best practices are important, but you still need to be prepared to put in plenty of hard work to grow your community and make it flourish.

---

1   www.sharetribe.com/booklinks, #1.
Throughout the book, we will regularly refer to online sources and articles for further reading. We have collected all these links for you on www.sharetribe.com/booklinks. There you can find the right link with the number indicated in the footnote, in this case "#1".

This first chapter will act as a high-level overview of the many things that are required to build a successful marketplace. These include:

- Why marketplaces are booming
- The most common challenges in building a marketplace business
- Why it's important to understand your personal motivation
- Why the best way to learn is by launching as soon as possible
- Why engaging your users should be a priority

We are going to take a deeper dive into these subjects in the following chapters.

Why marketplaces make for great businesses

The first time we came across Airbnb, we were amazed. The design and usability were excellent. Whenever we showed the service to someone, they fell in love with it. Many started searching for a host for their next trip right away. Once they returned from their trip, they recommended Airbnb to their friends and colleagues.

Airbnb is a poster child of the *sharing economy* (sometimes also called *collaborative economy*), a phenomenon where individuals and small businesses interact with each other directly through online marketplace platforms, bypassing the big corporations that traditionally acted as middlemen.

Many entrepreneurs who approach us are eager to share their idea of creating an "Airbnb for X". That's normal: the success of Airbnb and the sharing economy in general is something that cannot go unnoticed. And we're still talking about a young industry with great potential for growth. The consulting company PriceWaterhouseCoopers recently estimated that in the UK alone, the sharing economy generated transactions worth £28B[2] in 2015. They believe that in 2025, the same figure will be £140B, and Europe's total will reach €570B. Globally, this means the market will be worth more than a trillion.

---

2   www.sharetribe.com/booklinks, #2

The main reason online marketplace businesses scale so well is that you don't need to have your own inventory to run one. Airbnb does not own any hotel rooms, but it's already considered one of the biggest companies providing short term accommodation in the world. Uber is the world's largest taxi company without owning any cars. This is a really attractive proposition: you can build a huge business without having to spend a lot of money to buy the initial inventory, and thus taking on a lot of risk.

When Cristóbal started looking into how to build a marketplace platform in late 2009, the concept of the sharing economy didn't yet exist. Airbnb was virtually unknown and Uber had not yet launched. The most well-known marketplace websites were Ebay, Craigslist, and Couchsurfing. In less than 10 years, the market has changed completely as thousands of entrepreneurs are building the next generation of online marketplaces in multiple different sectors.

Building a successful marketplace is hard

Convincing people from all over the world to sleep in private residences was certainly not easy for Airbnb. These words from Airbnb's CEO Brian Chesky are a perfect illustration of what it took:

– *We met all these investors and they just wouldn't invest. So we started funding it ourselves. We sold collectible breakfast cereal and did other crazy things... We went door to door with cameras taking pictures of all these apartments to put them online. I lived in their living rooms. And home by home, block by block, communities started growing.*[3]

Building a successful marketplace business takes a lot of work. Coming up with an idea and launching the technology platform is just the very beginning. While you don't need to have your own inventory, you need to solve the chicken and egg problem: how to convince others to bring their inventory to your marketplace when there are still no buyers, and how to attract buyers

---

3   www.sharetribe.com/booklinks, #3

when you don't have inventory (yet). In chapter 11, we'll go over the different ways of overcoming this issue.

Your idea will also likely require a large-scale change in mindset. That's certainly the case with Airbnb. Before they started, most people hadn't thought of staying at the homes of unfamiliar people, or renting out their own bedroom to strangers. Airbnb managed to change that mindset, but it required a lot of time and effort in building an extremely convenient solution to find accommodation. Marketplaces are rarely overnight successes—most of them require patience to reach critical mass.

Understand your goals

Before you get busy developing your marketplace, you should take some time to reflect on three things: *why*, *what*, and *how*.

Why do you want to create a marketplace business? Is it because you are tired of working for another company? Perhaps you want to save the world, make tons of money, or build a profitable side business. Whatever the reasons are, articulating your true motivations for being an entrepreneur is important because your strategy will depend on them.

If your plan is to build a small business and eventually support yourself and maybe a small staff, it might make sense to focus on a smaller market. If, instead, you plan to build the next Airbnb and expect to raise money from venture capitalists, your market needs to be huge. As prolific marketplace investor Boris Wertz says about the investment strategy of his VC firm Version One Ventures:

– *We only invest in businesses that we believe can become really big. In the case of marketplaces, this means that we need to see the potential for $1B in annual Gross Merchandise Volume (the total amount of transactions going through your marketplace).*[4]

---

4   www.sharetribe.com/booklinks, #4

The next step is to figure out *what* it is that you're planning to build. Are you passionate about a particular idea, or on the lookout for a profitable niche? Our second chapter will focus on this topic, but it's important to keep in mind that building a marketplace requires a lot of dedication. The more passionate you are about your field, the more likely you are to succeed.

Finally, you need to figure out *how* to build your marketplace platform. Do you know how to write code? If not, do you have money to hire developers? Do you have previous experience running a startup? Do you have previous experience in the target market? Do you have co-founders or are you alone? The answers to these questions will help you define the best strategy for developing your idea. We recommend being pragmatic, and taking into account both your strengths and weaknesses—your professional experience, education, initial contacts and financial resources. These will influence the way you should start your business.

Most great startups are built by really capable teams of founders. However, if you do not have a skilled team around you (yet) but still want to shoot for the moon, worry not—there are ways to move forward with your business even if you are a sole founder without technical skills. In some cases, these constraints can actually work to your advantage.

Create your Minimum Viable Platform

While software development is relevant to the success of your marketplace, it is not enough to make it successful. We have seen many cases of entrepreneurs putting all their initial resources in the development of their platform, and then realizing that nobody is interested in using it. We call marketplaces that are technologically well built but fail at attracting users "desert platforms".

During the initial phase of the project, your main goal should be to develop a Minimum Viable Platform (MVP) and launch it as soon as possible. This will help you validate your marketplace idea without having to take a big risk and investing lots of capital. The learning process only starts once you have something to offer your users, so it's important to get to that point as soon as possible. Your first product needs to have just enough features to be able to solve your users' core problem.

We will go into more details on how to build an MVP in a later chapter, but one thing you should not focus on in the beginning is creating a perfect platform. We've met several entrepreneurs who want to develop a platform that works just as smoothly Airbnb already during the pre-launch phase, with all the same functionality. Having a long-term vision is important, but all successful platforms were Minimum Viable Platforms in the beginning.

For example, Airbnb started out with a basic WordPress site. Most of their current features were built only once they had proven that their basic concept works. You don't need to think about scaling to millions of users right away—instead, you should focus on finding 10 people who are really passionate about your concept.

One of the most common mistakes entrepreneurs make is spending too much time and financial resources on developing the platform before they launch. Instead, they should be doing a manual-first startup[5]—manually handling the tasks that will be automated by software later on.

Engage your users

Finally, one last thing we want to highlight in this overview is the importance of interacting with your users as soon as you start working on your project. Christopher Lukezic of Airbnb explains this well in this interview. When asked for advice he would give to a sharing economy entrepreneur, his response was:

> – *What I've learned from [the Airbnb founders] is to listen to your users early on and engage them in the process at every step of the way. Don't just meet them; engage them, converse with them, and prod them to find out what their problems and needs are. People often start companies to solve their own problems, but, over time, all entrepreneurs recognize*

---

5   www.sharetribe.com/booklinks, #5

that, to be successful, the product has to be built for a wider array of end users.[6]

— The ones who are truly successful make sure to engage their users at every point along the way in order to solve bigger and bigger problems by presenting transformative solutions to the way we live our lives.

Talking to your users can take a lot of time, but it's time that you simply need to spend. The platform you're building is an important piece of the puzzle, but it's your users and their level of engagement that really makes or breaks your business.

_____

6   www.sharetribe.com/booklinks, #6

2

How to come up with
a great marketplace idea

Perhaps you already have a business idea that you can't get out of your mind. Or maybe you are excited about the potential of the sharing economy, and are currently exploring different ideas. In either case, we assume that you're interested in building a successful marketplace business with thousands of users.

According to the startup playbook[7] by Sam Altman, four things are critical for success: the idea, the product, the team and the execution. The same basic principles apply whether you're building a global business, a local co-operative, or a non-profit. Everything starts from the idea.

In this chapter, we are going to cover the following topics:

- Why you need to solve a tangible problem
- How to find the right market
- How to improve existing solutions by adding a layer of trust
- Why it's important to narrow your focus
- How to do market research

---

7   www.sharetribe.com/booklinks, #7

Solve a real problem for your users

When we meet aspiring entrepreneurs, they are usually very excited about their idea and have a global vision for their concept. At the same time, they usually have a much harder time defining what the value proposition is for their users or what their strategy for gaining traction is.

When someone has a marketplace idea, they tend to describe how great it is when everyone uses their platform. Let's take the most common sharing economy example: a marketplace where people from all over the world share tools with their neighbors. This concept is easily relatable—most people want to live in a world where things are shared with each other. Everyone will tell you they love the idea. Unfortunately, this is not enough to make them actually use the service. If they are not in need of tools right now, or find it too cumbersome to share theirs, you are not solving a problem for them with your tool-sharing marketplace.

In the report Sharing is the New Buying: How to Win in the Collaborative Economy[8], marketplace expert Jeremiah Owyang shows that most people use peer-to-peer marketplaces for the same reasons they consume products in general: to get a cheaper price, better quality, or for convenience. People may claim that sustainability and a sense of community are important values to them, but these values do not necessarily guide their actions. If the thing they need is expensive, or the quality is bad, or it's not accessible, then that's a real problem.

---

8   www.sharetribe.com/booklinks, #8

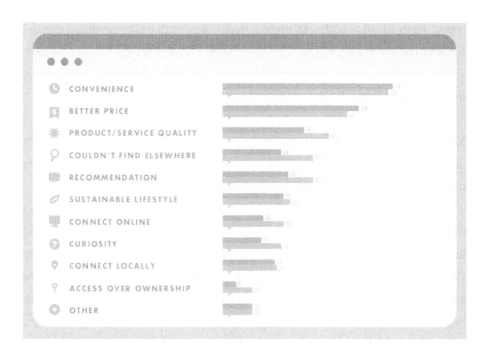

Reasons why people participate in the sharing economy. Source: Sharing is the New Buying:
How to Win in the Collaborative Economy by Crowd Companies and Vision Critical

Airbnb is a great example of a marketplace that started by solving such a problem: offering accommodation and breakfast for conference attendees who were unable to book a hotel (due to all of them being sold out) when they came to the IDSA design conference held in San Francisco in October of 2007.

Cristóbal experienced the importance of addressing the right problem first-hand while using the popular ridesharing service BlaBlaCar. At some point, he had to travel from Seville to Badajoz to give a talk. Finding a train or coach that fit his schedule was impossible, so he found a ride through BlaBlaCar instead. He talked to his fellow passengers and had a great experience during the round trip. They told him they use the platform because coaches and trains are more expensive, and their routes and schedules are not flexible enough. A report from BlaBlaCar[9] backs up this experience with data: members use the car-sharing service mainly because it's cheaper than other mobility services.

Not solving a real problem is one of the most common reasons for marketplace failure. Make sure your marketplace does not fall into this trap.

How can you be sure you have found a problem that is worth solving? Marketplaces are particularly tricky since you need to solve a problem for both sides: the customer and the provider. In other words, solving one big problem might not be enough—typically you will need to solve two.

Even if money is not always the best measure, it can be a good exercise to think about the size of the problem in terms of cash. How much would you be willing to pay someone if they solved the problem for you? This is why the sharing economy marketplaces that deal with high-value items generally fare better. Getting access to a car when you need it is a lot more valuable than being able to borrow a power drill.

As Sam Altman notes, the best validation usually happens after you've launched something that people can use. This is why it's a good idea to launch as early as possible. However, there are also things you can—and should—do before building your first product. We'll cover these ideas about validating your idea in chapter six.

Unlock idle assets

A strategy many successful marketplaces use is unlocking the economic value of underutilized assets. Vincent Rosso, former manager for Spain and Portugal at BlaBlaCar, explains the potential of the platform of BlaBlaCar as follows: "Every day, there are around 100-120 million empty car seats in Spain". BlaBlaCar's mission is to fill up these seats with passengers, using the car in a more efficient manner. According to sharing economy thought leader Robin Chase[10], the purpose of any marketplace platform is "[...] to liberate

---

9   www.sharetribe.com/booklinks, #9
10   www.sharetribe.com/booklinks, #10

the value hidden in excess capacity by engaging others: their assets, time, expertise and creativity."

It's time to put on your "sharing glasses". Look at the world around you. Try to find excess capacity, underutilized resources and assets that are not being used in an efficient way. Think of your work and your hobbies. Do you work in theater? Maybe a marketplace for renting out costumes. Are you a teacher? A marketplace for selling your teaching material. Do you coach junior hockey? A marketplace for selling used skates and other equipment. Do you like gardening? Build a marketplace for sharing plants and seeds! The opportunities are everywhere.

Jeremiah Owyang explains how marketplaces impact all areas of our society through the Collaborative Economy Honeycomb[11]. The first version only had six types of marketplace categories, but the latest version (at the time of writing this book) already contained sixteen. It seems inevitable that even more will be added in the future.

---

11   www.sharetribe.com/booklinks, #11

Collaborative Economy Honeycomb Version 3.0

The Collaborative Economy enables people to get what they need from each other. Similarly, in nature, honeycombs are resilient structures that enable access, sharing, and growth of resources among a common group.

In the original Honeycomb 1.0, six distinct categories of startups were represented by the inner track of hexes. After a short period of time, Honeycomb 2.0 expanded to include six additional categories, placed on the outer perimeter.

In the new Honeycomb 3.0, four hexes are added on the corners of the graphic for a total of sixteen: Beauty, Analytics & Reputation, Worker Support, and the large Transportation hex is split into two distinct hexes.

By Jeremiah Owyang
jeremiah@CrowdCompanies.com
@jowyang, March 2016

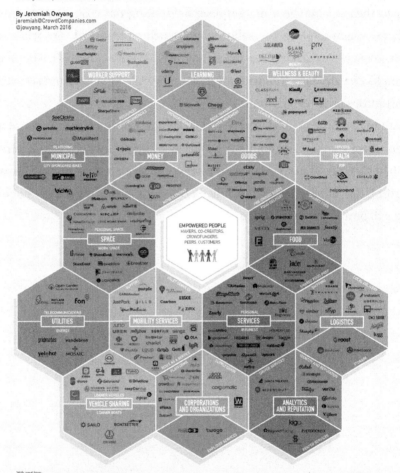

With input from:
Carl Bohlin, Matt Case, John Cass, Emily Castor, Shelby Clark, Lisa Gansky, Julie George, Neal Gorenflo, Greg Hedges, Bill Johnston, Karen Khoundhavong, Alex Lassar, Gregory Leproux, Angus Nelson, Andreas Pages, Shervin Pishevar, Augie Ray, April Rinne, Jeff Redman, Alexandra Samuel, Jamie Sandford, John Sheldon, Arun Sundararajan, Brian Solis, Julie Viola, Mike Walsh, Jonathan Wichmann, and Vision Critical.

Design by Vladimir Mirkovic www.transartdesign.com Creative Commons License: Attribution-NonCommercial.

CROWD COMPANIES
www.crowdcompanies.com

Collaborative Economy Honeycomb 3.0 by Crowd Companies[12]

By studying the honeycomb you can find new potential markets. The hottest startups have emerged in transportation, goods, space, and money, but there are still plenty of opportunities for solutions in other areas such as utilities, health, wellness, corporations, and municipalities. We're still in the early days of the marketplace industry.

Look for fragmented markets

Marketplaces are great at aggregating products or services into one place, and making them easily accessible and searchable by customers. Marketplaces thrive in areas where there are many small players offering their services instead of big, centralized providers.

Thumbtack has chosen the local professional services market, from plumbers to guitar teachers. Fiverr and Upwork cater to freelancers that provide digital services. Etsy helps individuals sell their custom-made crafts. These types of service providers have existed for a long time, but they lacked a central aggregator before the marketplaces came along.

From the customer's point of view, the marketplace offers a one-stop shop: a place to find all the providers and easily compare them. From the provider's point of view, the marketplace brings them more clients. Both parties get their problems solved. Everyone wins.

Improve an existing solution by adding a layer of trust

There's nothing new in the real-world encounters that these marketplaces facilitate. Hitchhiking, selling second hand clothes, borrowing tools, and sharing apartments were common practices long before the new wave of marketplace startups emerged. What's new in the modern solutions is how easy it is to interact with strangers.

Years ago, Cristóbal used the classifieds marketplace Loquo (the Barcelonian version of Craigslist) to find rooms from shared apartments in Barcelona. He remembers only choosing listings that had pictures. He was also very picky about the way the posts were written. Loquo didn't have a reputation system, so he had to rely on intuition to decide if the apartment would be worth visiting and whether his potential roommates would be nice. Finding a room through Loquo was a tedious process: it required a lot of dedication to filter through the listings and visit potential apartments to find a suitable one.

The experience with Airbnb is totally different. You can see apartment reviews, the hosts have verifications, and even our mutual Facebook friends are displayed. Airbnb has brought trust to a market where there previously was none, and because of that, they're making the experience a lot more pleasant for everyone.

Sangeet Choudary of Platform Thinking Labs explains how Craigslist is facing a threat from the new players that are disrupting its verticals one by one:

> – *Ironically, Craigslist, the king of liquidity, doesn't have a reliable method of determining a user's reputation. While this may be acceptable for certain categories (e.g. selling low-value goods), it can be an important decision criterion for categories with high risk (e.g. babysitters, dating, apartment sharing) or high ticket investment (e.g. trading used high-end goods).*[13]

Craigslist is being disrupted by Airbnb in apartments, Etsy in custom-made goods, Thumbtack in local services, BlaBlaCar in ridesharing, and so on. All these new players use elaborate reputation systems to build trust and make sure things go smoothly.

---

13   www.sharetribe.com/booklinks, #13

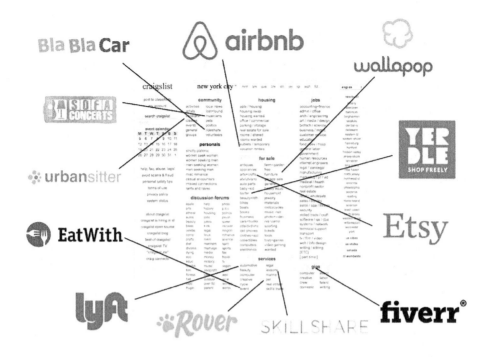

How modern marketplace startups are disrupting Craigslist category by category.

If you are looking to start a marketplace, studying Craigslist categories is a great way to understand niche markets and find ideas. The more listings there are in a certain category, the bigger the demand. Can you find a category where there does not seem to be enough trust between providers? That category might be your opportunity.

How do you design a reputation system and build trust? That's an important question, and one that we'll get back to in a later chapter.

Have a narrow focus

Classifieds marketplaces like Craigslists and Loquo are horizontal platforms: they facilitate exchanges in multiple different categories, like jobs, ridesharing, services, buying and selling stuff, renting apartments, and so on. In contrast, Airbnb is a typical example of a vertical platform. It focuses on one core problem: finding temporary accommodation.

The vertical platforms have an advantage. Since they focus on only one thing, they are often able to do it extremely well. They can build their platform solely around the one problem their users have, and thus provide a great experience.

Along with not solving the right problem, another common reason why marketplaces fail is having too broad a focus. A narrow focus is especially important during the early days of your business, when your resources are limited.

When we talk to successful marketplace founders, we always ask them about the biggest mistakes they've made. Their answer is almost always the same: they tried scaling too quickly, either by vertical or by geography. Thus, we strongly recommend you to focus your marketplace on one city and one vertical and only scale when you've truly proven that your concept is working.

Being focused has many benefits. It's much easier to build a product for a specific target group. You can tailor your message and your features with only that group in mind. If you choose a narrow vertical, it will also be a lot easier to achieve critical mass in that vertical. If your marketplace is about sharing all kinds of tools everywhere in the world, someone looking for a jackhammer in France will likely be disappointed. If you focus only on sharing jackhammers in Detroit, it's quite likely that your customers will find what they're looking for.

When working with early stage entrepreneurs, having too broad a focus is a problem that we run into time and again. Convincing the founders to narrow their focus is always a challenge because it goes against their intuition. Having a slightly broader focus can be a good early-stage strategy to find your niche, but once it has been found, focusing on one product or service vertical is the way to go for the majority of marketplaces. It's often helpful to think about how the biggest companies got started. Amazon started by only selling books. Airbnb started by offering accommodation to designers who were attending a specific conference in San Francisco.

Do you have a great idea for a marketplace but feel there's already too much competition in that market? One strategy is to narrow your focus, both geographically and in terms of the offered products or services. You might not want to compete with Airbnb on building a global platform for temporary accommodation, but perhaps focusing only on renting summer cottages in Finland or castles in France might bring you your competitive advantage.

You can always broaden your focus later on, once you get the initial vertical going. ThredUP first started with too broad a focus, and after failing to gain traction, they narrowed it down to focus only on kids' clothes. Once they were successful in that segment, they extended their offering to adults as well. Knok started as a general home exchange platform and pivoted to focus only on families. Later on, they scaled their offering to home exchange, apartment rentals and local guides to the families as well.

We expect that as the costs of building marketplace businesses go down, we are going to see more and more specialized marketplaces that excel in serving very specific user segments and geographies. Not all of them will be the size of Airbnb, but that should not always be the goal—it's often enough to build a solid, sustainable business and focus on serving your core users. A good example of this type of niche marketplace is Behomm, a home exchange community for creatives and design lovers.

See what others are doing

After you come up with a great idea, the next natural step is market research: is someone already doing the same thing? We have met many entrepreneurs who state they are "the first marketplace that allows people to share clothes from their wardrobes" or "the first marketplace for sharing idle equipment between companies" when, in fact, similar marketplaces already exist.

If your idea is any good, it is quite likely that someone else is already working on the same thing. The best ideas usually come to multiple people at once. Do not be discouraged by this. In the end, execution is what counts. As was discussed above, one good way to combat competition is to narrow your focus, either geographically or by segment.

Even though you should not be discouraged by competition, it is still important to take a quick look at the market to see how others are trying to solve the same problem you have identified. To do this efficiently, using some kind of methodology is recommended. The below is Cristóbal's approach when looking for information about competitors or similar projects. In this case, he was working with the team of a marketplace for yoga teachers that he used to advise:

First, he used Google to find initial information about similar initiatives and potential competitors.

This led him to a competitor targeting yoga centers and teachers. He concluded that their supply was built upon databases. He also discovered two other interesting and successful projects that gave his team insights to help define their strategy. It's a good idea to build a list of all the search queries you can come up with, and go through the results one by one.

He then wanted to find out more about the history of these companies.

He used Google's date interval feature to find news articles from past years with relevant information about their strategy and pivots. Using this feature, he found out that one of the companies had changed their name and had a decisive pivot in their business model.

Next, he wanted to learn more about their teams and funding situation.

AngelList and CrunchBase are convenient databases for finding this type of information. The information you will find on these sites is not 100% accurate, but it will still give you a rough idea about the state of the companies. For instance, he found out that one company had just raised an initial seed fund round.

He finally made searches in marketplace directories.

There are quite a few directories out there: collaborative consumption directory, mesh directory, honeycomb 3.0 from Jeremiah Owyang and consumo colaborativo directory for Spanish and Latin American projects.[14]

Talk about your idea with everyone

As said, if your idea is any good, you can expect others to be working on the idea as well. This means that you should not be afraid of talking about your idea with others. On the contrary; you should talk about it with everyone you know. As Sam Altman points out:

– *You don't need to be too secretive with your idea. There are at least a thousand times more people that have good ideas than people who are willing to do the kind of work it takes to turn a great idea into a great company. And if you tell people what you're doing, they might help.*

Sharing your idea with others is a great way to get relevant feedback, and perhaps hear about related projects. Share your idea with friends and family, the people in your coworking space, the people you meet in networking events, the people you meet at a nightclub, anyone and anywhere. Cristóbal remembers being in a party in Paris when someone was excited to introduce him to the founder of WhereIsMyMat just because he knew Cristóbal was working on the marketplace for yoga teachers mentioned before. If nobody is familiar with your business, they won't be able to help you.

It might also be a good idea to contact the other companies in your field. This lets you learn more about them, understand their strengths and weaknesses, and have a better idea of where you should focus on.

---

14   www.sharetribe.com/booklinks, #14, #15, #12, #16

Summary

Finding a great idea is a critical step in building a sustainable marketplace business. You should make sure that you're solving a real, painful problem for both the customers and providers of your marketplace with this idea. In the early days, it's especially important to focus on a narrow niche to that mission.

Many great marketplace ideas are based on unlocking idle assets or aggregating small providers from fragmented markets. In many cases, you can improve on the existing solutions by building a layer of trust with your marketplace.

Once you have come up with an idea, research the field to find out what others are doing. If your idea is any good, others are likely working on it as well. Don't be discouraged—instead, talk about your idea openly to everyone and try to find a unique angle and strategy to focus on.

Already have a great idea? Great, let's move forward and start designing the business model of your marketplace.

3

How to choose the right business model

Marketplace businesses are long-term initiatives. To build a sustainable and successful marketplace, you need to find a revenue stream that will finance its operations.

If you are running a non-profit or a hobby project, funding the development and maintenance of the site can be done through donations or from your own pocket. However, in most cases, funding eventually needs to come from the community you are serving—the users of your site.

One of the most common reasons why startups fail is that they pick a business model that does not scale to ensure long-term sustainability. In this chapter, we review different options for marketplace monetization, and give guidance on how to choose the right model for your idea.

Commission

The most popular revenue stream for modern marketplaces is to charge a commission from each transaction. When a customer pays a provider, the marketplace facilitates the payment and charges either a percentage or a flat fee.

The biggest benefit of this model is that providers are not charged anything before they get some value from the marketplace. This is a really attractive model for the providers, as the money they pay is directly aligned with the value they get. At the same time, from the marketplace's point of view, this model is usually the most lucrative: you get a piece of all the value that passes through your platform. The best known marketplace platforms—Airbnb, Etsy, eBay, Fiverr, TaskRabbit and Uber—all use commissions as their main business model.

The biggest challenge in getting the commission model to work is to provide enough value for both the customer and the provider. If your users do not get enough value from your platform, they will find a way to circumvent your payment system, and you will not get paid. How do you prevent this phenomenon (often called *disintermediation*)? We'll dive into that question in the next chapter.

Another challenge with the commission model is the commission structure. How big should the commission be? Should it be the same for all users? Should I charge the customer, the provider, or both? Should I first have a lower commission to get people to join my platform, and raise it later on? We'll dedicate chapter five to these questions.

Our recommendation is to use the commission model as your main revenue stream whenever possible. Especially if you're targeting a narrow niche, the commission model is often the only way to ensure sufficient revenue[15]. We anticipate more and more marketplaces adopting this model in the future.

There are, however, scenarios in which it is not feasible for the marketplace to facilitate payment transaction. In these cases, the commission model does not work. Examples include:

- When the size of the typical transaction is huge. With car or real estate sales, for instance, it's difficult for the marketplace to justify the commission.

---

15   www.sharetribe.com/booklinks, #17

- The marketplace has many different types of offerings. It becomes impossible to design a transaction process that provides value for all of those cases. Traditional classified ads are a good example of this.
- The invoicing process is too complex for the marketplace to facilitate it. This is common in business-to-business (B2B) and some business-to-consumer (B2C) marketplaces.
- Money is not exchanged at all in the marketplace. For instance, if the marketplace is about dating, finding people to hire, bartering, or sharing something for free, there's no monetary transaction involved, and thus no way to charge a commission.

In these cases, you need a different type of revenue stream. Below are some examples of other possible revenue models.

Membership or subscription fee

A membership fee (sometimes called a subscription fee) is a model where either some or all of a marketplace's users are charged a recurring fee to access the marketplace. With this model, the typical value proposition for providers is that the marketplace helps them find new customers. For customers, it helps them save costs or find unique experiences.

The membership fee is a good choice if the value you provide is high and a typical user will engage in several transactions, but facilitating a payment is challenging or impossible.

Typical examples of consumer-to-consumer (C2C) marketplaces with membership fees are home swapping sites (Love Home Swap, Home Exchange) and dating sites (OkCupid, Match.com). Oftentimes, these sites vet all the subscribers in order to guarantee quality matches and create a sense of exclusivity that justifies the fee.

In the B2C market, the membership model is common in recruiting. For instance, LinkedIn and StackOverflow Careers charge companies a subscription fee to get access to their talent pools. Studiotime, an "Airbnb for record studios", is an example of another niche where membership fees work as the main business model. With B2C companies, the platform is typically free for customers, but requires a paid subscription for providers.

A membership fee can also be a good initial business model for B2C marketplaces that eventually want to charge a commission but don't yet have the tools in place to facilitate transactions in their particular niche. Venuu, an "Airbnb for event spaces", started with the membership model in order to get revenue upfront, even before launching their site. Later on, when they had validated their business plan and had the resources to build an invoicing system, they moved to the commission model—a model that was much more lucrative for them. Studiotime used a similar strategy.

The challenge with the membership fee model is that it makes the "chicken and egg problem"—how to find providers without customers and how to find customers without providers—even worse. You need to have enough users on your platform to make it valuable for both providers and customers, and a mandatory payment discourages users from signing up. One way to get around this is to offer heavy discounts for early adopters, or even lift the fee completely to build the initial user base.

Listing fee

Some marketplaces charge a fee from providers when they post new listings. This model is typically used when providers get value based on the number of listings they have on the site, and the potential value per listing is big.

This model is quite common with classified ads. The value proposition of the website is very simple: it aggregates a massive volume of listings into a single online destination, and guarantees lots of visibility for those listings. Classified ad platforms typically don't even try to facilitate the transaction.

Perhaps the most well-known example in this category is Craigslist. It is a collection of local sites where people can post listings about anything they want, whether it's about selling goods, services, jobs, finding an apartment, dating, or something else. Generally, posting a new listing to Craigslist is free—this is how they managed to reach critical user mass—but in certain categories (namely, job and apartment listings in some cities) they charge a fee for each listing.

It can sometimes be useful to use several business models on the same site. For instance, Etsy is an example of a B2C marketplace that uses the commission model, but also charges a fee to post new listings. Etsy's reasoning for this is likely that its *sell-through rate* (the probability of a certain item being sold) is not as high as it wants it to be. While there are some hugely popular items on Etsy, most items likely never get a single sale because Etsy's total volume of listings is massive. By using both the commission model and the listing fee model, Etsy gets revenue from both popular and not so popular items.

A listing fee is better than a membership fee in cases where providers don't want a continuous subscription, and only want to sell a few items or sell for a short period of time. This is the case with Mascus, a B2B classifieds site for expensive machinery.

The challenge with the listing fee model is that it doesn't guarantee value for providers, and thus the fee cannot be too high. This results in the marketplace being able to capture only a relatively small portion of the value going through the site. A sustainable business model that depends solely on listing fees thus requires a very large volume of listings. Additionally, since paying a listing fee does not guarantee that the item is sold, the marketplace will have a harder time proving that it provides actual value to its providers.

Lead fee

The lead fee model is somewhere between the listing fee and commission models. In a typical lead fee model, customers post requests on the site, and providers pay in order to make a bid for these customers. The model gives a better value proposition than the listing fee model: you only pay when you are put in touch with a potential customer.

The lead fee model only works if the value of the lead is high. For this reason, this model is not common in C2C marketplaces. A typical use case is B2C or B2B services, where each new lead can lead to a long-lasting customer relationship with multiple deals. A recent well-performing example of this model is Thumbtack, a B2C marketplace for all kinds of local professional services, from plumbers to guitar teachers. The fast-growing startup was recently valued at more than $1 billion[16].

However, while Thumbtack has been doing well with the lead fee model so far, their challenge is that providers stop using Thumbtack with existing customers—instead, they build the relationship outside the platform once they have the lead. This is why Thumbtack has said it's going to build invoicing, payment and scheduling tools for professionals. Thumbtack is likely to eventually move towards the commission model to extract more value from the transactions they help facilitate.

Freemium

How can you monetize a marketplace where people share low-value items for free? The Dutch startup Peerby built a C2C platform where people can borrow things from each other at no cost. The basic experience is free for all the users of the platform. Peerby monetizes by offering premium services. They have two main offerings: insurance (the provider can request that the customer, while getting the item for free, pays an insurance fee that guarantees the item will be replaced if it is damaged or stolen) and delivery (the customer can pay a small fee to get the item delivered to their door instead of having to go pick it up from the provider).

The logic behind the freemium model is that the core offering is free, but after you get your users hooked, you offer paid value-adding features. The challenge with this model is that these paid services need to provide enough value to be tempting to a good portion of your users. If only 1% of your users are interested in your premium offering and everyone else uses your site for free, it's probably not enough for a sustainable business model. Coming up

---

16   www.sharetribe.com/booklinks, #18

with a premium service that is interesting for a wide enough audience can be very tricky.

Because of this, many platforms use premium services as additional revenue streams. For example, Mascus offers premium web page services to complement its listing fee based business model. Etsy complements its transaction and listing fee based model by offering premium services like direct checkout, listing promotion and shipping labels to its power sellers, and has recently seen strong growth from this revenue stream.

In some cases, a marketplace can start offering premium services as an add-on, but eventually shift its entire business model to focus on the paid services. Vayable started as a pure peer-to-peer marketplace where individual people offer unique experiences to others, but after failing to get enough traction, decided to pivot to build a concierge service for custom vacations.

The downside of the freemium approach is that premium services are often be a less scalable option when compared to the pure commission model. This is often due to the amount of staff that is required to provide premium services. Vayable only made the shift because they were unable to get the commission model off the ground.

Featured listings and ads

Featured listings are a way for providers to buy more visibility for their offerings. If this model is used, listing on the site is typically free, but providers can pay to have their listing be featured on the homepage of the site, or at the top of a certain category. An example of this model is Gumtree, UK's most popular classified ads website. Etsy provides featured listings as one of its premium services.

This model is relatively close to pure advertising models—ones where you show ads (such as Google AdSense) to your users. Featured listings and ads are both popular revenue streams for classified ad sites. They are often seen on real estate marketplaces (like Zillow) or free sharing marketplaces (like Freecycle).

The challenge with these models is that, again, they require a significant amount of users to generate meaningful revenue. When you're in the business of selling eyeballs, the revenue you generate per user is likely a lot less than if you can extract value from your transaction process. Moreover, when you're placing ads on your site, you're serving two audiences with conflicting interests: from a user experience point of view, ads are almost always a hindrance, and your users would generally be happier without ads. If you want to offer the best possible experience for your users, this business model is not your best option.

Ad-based models work best when you have a really specific niche, and there are commercial providers that are interested in tailoring their offering for that specific audience. For instance, Häätori, a Finnish wedding marketplace for used wedding dresses, lets individuals use the site for free. They monetize by allowing wedding planners, photographers and other providers of wedding-related services to buy ads on the site. The content of these ads is very relevant for the users of the website, making them more relevant and less annoying.

Summary

Modern marketplaces employ many different business models. In general, the best option for most marketplaces is to "own the transaction" and charge a commission from all purchases made through the site. This approach is very scalable and oftentimes quite lucrative.

However, in some cases, the commission model does not make sense, so alternative models are needed.

Trying out multiple business models to find the best option for your concept might be a good idea. In the beginning, you should have only one revenue stream in use at a time to avoid diverting your focus. Eventually, when your site grows, it might make sense to combine several revenue streams to build a business model that takes into account everything that is happening on your site.

4

How to avoid disintermediation

As we learned in the previous chapter, the most lucrative revenue stream for a modern marketplace is to "own" the entire purchase and payment process and charge a commission from each transaction.

The commission model works well because you receive a chunk of all the value going through your site. However, the flip side of this is that the more value you extract, the more value you need to provide your users in the process. If you fail to provide enough value, users will find ways to circumvent your payment system to avoid your fees. This is called *disintermediation* or *platform leakage*, and it's a challenge faced by many marketplace founders— even sometimes causing marketplaces to go out of business[17].

Avoid disintermediation by providing value in the transaction

How can you avoid disintermediation? Since we're dealing with two-sided marketplaces, you have two parties in each transaction: the provider (the party providing the product or the service) and the customer (the party receiving the product or the service). You need to consider how to *provide value in the transaction* for both sides.

---

17   www.sharetribe.com/booklinks, #19

The best strategy depends a lot on your particular concept. Does your marketplace deal with high-value or low-value items? Is it about selling products, renting them out, or providing services? Is the marketplace consumer-to-consumer (C2C), business-to-consumer (B2C), or business-to-business (B2B)?

In this chapter, we will go through the most common ways to provide value for both parties in the transaction.

The value for individuals offering products or services: Security

If your providers are individuals, the best way to provide value is to focus on trust and safety. People are hesitant to trust strangers. If I am renting my car or power drill to a stranger, how can I be sure they will not steal it, trash it, or break it? This distrust creates lots of friction in C2C marketplaces. The marketplace itself can reduce friction by acting as a trusted middleman.

Simply having a formal contract between parties can sometimes be enough to offer a sense of security. The customer needs to accept the terms of a rental marketplace when making a booking. In these terms, the marketplace can lay out what happens in case of fraud or damaged goods. If the customer violates these terms, they can face legal consequences in which the transaction can easily be proven.

If you have a rental marketplace that deals with high value items, you can offer insurance. If an item is stolen or broken, the insurance will cover it—but only if the payment was conducted through your marketplace's payment system. For example, ShareGrid, a peer-to-peer marketplace for professional camera rentals, has items worth more than $100,000 on their site, so insurance is a core value proposition for them.

Sometimes insuring the rented property is not enough. Peer-to-peer carsharing marketplace RelayRides prides on offering an insurance of up to $1 million, and it covers not only damage to the car, but also potential claims from third parties for damage or injuries. Unlike most of its competitors, BlaBlaCar charges a commission, and justifies it with ridesharing insurance that covers both drivers and passengers.

Marketplaces that deal with intangible services often provide value by offering guarantees. For instance, home cleaning marketplace Handy and legal service marketplace UpCounsel refund dissatisfied customers from their own pocket.

Marketplace insurance is a complex topic, and a deeper analysis on it is out of the scope of this book. If you want to dive deeper into the subject, we recommend the Insurance for Online Marketplaces eBook by Esther Val. It offers a thorough analysis for those considering insurance.

If you initially cannot afford to offer insurance or are unable to find an insurance company willing to tailor a suitable package for you, another option is to use a rental deposit. Essentially, the customer pays an upfront deposit that is returned to them if the item is not damaged. This is what Juho did when he rented a car from the French car-sharing platform Deways. He managed to test the insurance first-hand by accidentally scratching the rental car. Deways took some of his deposit money to pay for the car repair, and the rest was returned to him. The process was smooth, but the upfront deposit felt quite hefty. This can be an issue with deposits: people are wary of transferring large sums of money, while smaller deposits might not cover serious incidents.

If you are selling goods instead of renting them, you do not need to be concerned about items being damaged; you most likely don't care what happens to the item after receiving your money. However, there are other issues that can cause trouble for sellers, especially if they are shipping items. For instance, the buyer can claim they didn't receive an item, or that it was broken, and demand a refund. Or they can simply file a dispute with their credit card company and get their money back. This can be a big problem for the seller. The marketplace can mitigate this risk by handling all dispute situations to protect sellers. If you do not want to take on the financial risk related to this, you can leave it to your payment provider. PayPal, for instance, offers a comprehensive seller protection program.

Reputation systems are another way of providing security. eBay pioneered the practice of the buyer and the seller leaving each other feedback after a successful transaction. Both parties then have an incentive to behave well, since getting a bad rating might ruin their future transactions. Today, almost every successful marketplace uses a similar system.

A reputation system has an additional benefit for providers: it helps them sell more. Many studies have shown that eBay sellers with good reputations are able to charge higher prices than sellers of similar products with inferior ratings or no reviews. Airbnb hosts typically start with a lower price and increase it while building up their reputation. Since a review can usually only be given if the transaction happened through the marketplace's payment system, they are a great way to provide value in the transaction.

In service marketplaces, online payment in itself may provide security for providers. Uber is a prime example of this. A taxi driver is a likely target for a robbery because they are known to carry a lot of cash. With Uber, the monetary transaction happens online, eliminating the need to carry cash.

The value for professional service providers: Tools

If your service marketplace providers are professionals who make their entire living (or at least a substantial part of it) by providing said service, you may need to provide value in additional ways. Transactions in these marketplaces—for cleaners, dog sitter, guitar teachers—are typically recurring in nature: after a customer finds a provider they like, they're likely to use the provider's services again.

What often happens is that the first transaction goes through the marketplace, but the ensuing ones are handled through other channels. The reasons for this are obvious: the customer and the provider trust one another after the first successful transaction. They do not get additional value from the security provided by the marketplace. They have likely exchanged their contact information, and no longer need to communicate through the platform.

Since the provider can offer the customer a cheaper price—one without the marketplace commission—this option becomes quite tempting.

Marketplaces can be relatively successful by focusing on solely capturing the first transaction between customers and providers. However, there are strategies to capture subsequent ones as well.

One such strategy is to become a Software-as-a-Service tool for your providers[18]. Your marketplace is no longer just about acquiring new customers—you also help the providers run their business by automating mundane tasks.

Freelancer marketplace UpWork (previously oDesk and Elance) is a great example of this approach. From the point of view of a freelancer, getting a new gig requires many tedious tasks. They need to work on a proposal with the client, get their approval, agree on the compensation, invoice the customer, deliver the results, pay their taxes, and handle accounting. UpWork has created a smooth workflow for freelancers, automating all these steps. The freelancer saves a lot of time thanks to this process—enough for it to be worth the commission.

There are many different ways to provide value. If your providers need to deliver their services during an exact time (think hairdresser, cleaner, babysitter, or rental provider), you likely want to help them manage their availability with a scheduling feature. If the professionals are shipping goods (like on Etsy), you can help them manage their inventory and handle delivery. By providing good enough software tools, you can be an essential part of your provider's' business process, and your commission is a small price to pay for that level of service.

The value for customers: Reduce friction

From a customer's point of view, a marketplace's most important function is to make the transaction as smooth and easy as possible. There are many

---

18   www.sharetribe.com/booklinks, #20

different ways to do this: by removing steps from the transaction process, by removing the need to carry cash, and by increasing trust, for example.

Paying for something is always a hurdle. Studies have shown that if purchasing is easier, people will buy more. People may give up on a transaction simply because paying is too tedious.

If you're building a service marketplace, you should consider whether you can "productize"[19] the offered services with pre-defined scopes, durations and pricing. This reduces the required back and forth communication between the customer and provider, which means they're more likely to complete the transaction on your platform.

Airbnb initially built their payment system after the founder, Brian Chesky, had an awkward experience using the site: he was staying with a host he didn't know, and forgot to bring enough cash with him. When it came time to pay, he had to ask the host if he could go pick up some cash from an ATM. The trust between him and the host was broken. After Airbnb started offering online payments, the problem disappeared. The guest and the host no longer had to have the money conversation. Uber customers get a similar benefit: there is no need to ask the taxi driver to make an ATM stop.

If the payment is made in advance, the customer takes on the risk that the provider is a no-show or that they do not get the product they ordered. Again, the marketplace can help by becoming a middleman. An "escrow" service (sometimes also called "delayed payout") is one way to do this; the marketplace captures the payment and notifies the provider about it, but doesn't move the money to the provider before they have completed the service in question.

The challenge with escrow is that it is heavily regulated, and regulation varies by country. Before using escrow, it is a good idea to research the legislation specific to your country and industry. Luckily, many payment processors (like Stripe and MangoPay) nowadays offer solutions for delaying payouts as

---

19   www.sharetribe.com/booklinks, #21

a standard part of their offering, moving the regulatory responsibility away from the marketplace.

If you do not want to delay payouts, you have two alternatives. You can preauthorize the customer's credit card without charging it and keep the preauthorization until the money needs to be moved. This is enough in most cases. However, the longer the hold period, the bigger the risk that the money transfer fails when you finally initiate it. This would leave the provider in trouble.

The other alternative is to offer buyer's protection for cases where the provided service did not meet the buyer's needs or expectations. PayPal has buyers covered as well with their comprehensive buyer protection program.

Building a good reputation is important from a customer's point of view as well. Airbnb hosts use reviews as a vetting mechanism, and might only accept bookings from people with positive reviews. If the customer wants to build their reputation as a trusted guest, they need to use Airbnb's booking system. Customers are thus incentivized to pay through the platform in order to build their reputation.

Communication strategies

If you are unable to provide enough value in the transaction process, there are a few other strategies that might deter people from bypassing your payment system. However, none of them are bulletproof, and some of them can do more harm than good; use them with care. They are best used as a complement to the strategies discussed above.

One approach is to keep an open communication line with your users: remind them that commissions are what keep the site running, and if people bypass it, your site will disappear. Alternatively, instead of appealing to the good nature of your users, you can take a more draconian approach and remind users that those who bypass the system will be banned. Of course, this might not be the best way to build a sense of community.

You could also consider making it harder for people to exchange contact information before a transaction takes place. This approach is currently in use on a number of big platforms. Airbnb removes contact details (like email addresses and phone numbers) from private messages between users. It is, however, always possible to circumvent this limitation—by writing a phone number with letters, for instance. Airbnb says they do this to protect their users, but it is quite clear the underlying motive is to prevent users from bypassing their payment system. BlaBlaCar does not allow private messages before transactions at all; instead, all questions need to be asked publicly.

You can, of course, choose to not provide a pre-transaction messaging system for your users at all, but in most cases, this will simply not work. Customers may need to have a conversation with the provider before making a purchase decision. Putting excessive communication barriers in place will create friction on your site, annoy your users, and will likely lead to them abandoning your site.

As Andrei Hagiu and Simon Rothman write in their Harvard Business Review article on network effects:

> – *We've found that carrots are more effective deterrents than sticks. --- As long as a marketplace provides value, there should be sufficient incentive for one or both sides to conduct all their transactions through the platform. If users find it onerous to do so, then either the marketplace does not create enough value or its fees are too high[20].*

Offer providers a stake in your business

Thinking about your providers as partners is often a good strategy. Your goals and their goals should be aligned: if they win, you win. If you try to extract too much value without providing enough for them, this reciprocal relationship is shattered, and your business will ultimately fail. To be really

---

20   www.sharetribe.com/booklinks, #22

successful, a marketplace must get to a point where it has a loyal group of providers who feel that the best interests of the marketplace align with theirs.

One (perhaps radical) way to achieve this is to offer the providers a stake in your business. The most natural company structure for this is a provider-owned cooperative. What you might lose due to the slowed down decision-making—democracy takes time, after all—can be gained by having providers who are fully aligned with your goals, who promote your marketplace to everyone they know, who are more inclined to provide good service to your customers—and who will definitely not bypass your payment system.

If you are interested in this option, there is a whole movement, platform cooperativism[21], that is currently being built around this particular approach. One of the most well-known examples of platform cooperatives is stock photo marketplace Stocksy, a cooperative owned by the photographers. The cooperative model has allowed Stocksy to lure many professional photographers away from incumbent sites like Getty Images. In 2016, Stocksy grew its annual revenue to $10.7 million.

If you do not want to go down the cooperative route, there are other possible ways to set up your company. You can have a regular limited company and issue small amounts of shares to providers. You could also experiment with new technology. In 2014, the popular content community site Reddit announced plans to share 10% of their funding round ($5 million in total) with their users. Their plan was to utilize their own cryptocurrency powered by the blockchain protocol. While this is currently a rather complicated path to take, new technological innovations are constantly taking place and we will likely see such ownership distribution becoming a more viable option.

Summary

If you want to own the purchase process, you need to provide enough value in the transaction—both for the customer and the provider. If your providers

---

21   www.sharetribe.com/booklinks, #23

are individuals renting or selling products, you should focus on trust and security. If your providers are professionals, consider building tools that help them run their business. Make it as effortless as possible for your customers to make the purchase.

Your providers should be your partners. You can consider playing hardball and imposing communication-related limitations to make users behave well, but this approach can easily backfire since it breaches your relationship that is based on mutual trust. A likely better approach is to align your interest with your providers' by offering them a stake in your business.

5

How to set your commission

In the previous chapter, we explained how to discourage users from going around your payment system. In this chapter, we'll focus on your fee structure. What should be the size of your commission (sometimes called "transaction fee", "take rate" or "rake")—the portion of each sale that makes up your revenue?

At first, you might think that the correct answer is "as high as possible". However, as marketplace specialist Bill Gurley of legendary venture capital firm Benchmark states in his classic blog post "A Rake Too Far: Optimal Platform Pricing Strategy"[22], in some cases the exact opposite might be true.

Just like with business models, there is no single pricing strategy that works for all marketplaces. In this chapter, we will go through the most important aspects that affect marketplace pricing and help you choose the correct pricing strategy based on your specific marketplace concept.

What are others doing?

To get a baseline for pricing, let's examine what modern marketplaces are doing. On many popular service marketplaces like Uber, Fiverr, Lyft and

---

22   www.sharetribe.com/booklinks, #24

Postmates, the commission seems to hover around 20%. Some people have even claimed that 20% is the optimal commission for most new marketplaces[23].

Meanwhile, in product marketplaces, the story is quite different. Etsy is on the lower end, charging only 3.5%. eBay and Amazon hover around 10%. Rental marketplaces seem to have more variance, with Airbnb charging between 12% and 20% and Turo (previously RelayRides) between 10% and 35%.

Bill Gurley has created a handy table for comparing the different take rates of many successful marketplaces. The most important takeaway is that the variations are huge: from OpenTable's 1.9% to ShutterStock's 70%.

Company	Rake	Notes
Opentable	1.9%	Reservation fee / average meal per person
Homeaway	2.5%	Estimated (low due to use of listing model instead of transaction)
Comparison shopping	6.0%	Estimated
eBay	9.9%	This is partially listing fees, partially marketing fees, and part Paypal
oDesk	10.0%	10% on top of work billed
Airbnb	11.0%	3% + 6-12% depending on size of transaction
Expedia	11.9%	Per 2012 10-K
Amazon Marketplace	12.0%	Guess based on rate table
Fandango	12.5%	Fee charged to user / ticket price
PriceLine	18.5%	Per 2012 10-K
TicketMaster	26.0%	Estimate for tickets sold by TM (non box-office) - very hard to discern
Steam	30.0%	Rate card
iTunes	30.0%	Rate card
Facebook Credits	30.0%	Rate card
Groupon	38.2%	Calculated from 2012 10-K. Does not include direct goods.
Shutterstock	70.0%	From S-1

Table based on Bill Gurley's rake comparison table[24]

23   www.sharetribe.com/booklinks, #25
24   www.sharetribe.com/booklinks, #24

We also wanted to take a look at a larger dataset, so we studied the commissions of all marketplaces created with Sharetribe's marketplace platform. In November 2017, we found almost 15 000 marketplaces (including closed ones) that use or have used a commission as their business model. The average commission on these sites is 9%, with a median of 7%.

Is this a successful strategy? To find it out, we took a look at the 20 most successful Sharetribe customers in terms of monthly revenue. Their average commission was 14.7%, with the highest being 35% and lowest being 5%. The median was 15%, which was also the most common commission among them.

Based on this quick analysis, in order to be financially successful, you likely need to provide enough value to your users to justify a commission of at least 15%—but there's a lot of variation. As Gurley's table and the wide variety in the commissions show, going with an average is too simplified. Several factors need to be taken into consideration based on your specific type of marketplace business. We'll look at these factors next.

Factors that affect marketplace pricing

We are going to take a look at seven factors that affect the final pricing decision: marginal costs, competition, network effects, provider differentiation, transaction size and volume, quality vs quantity, and who pays the bill.

Marginal costs

The most important thing to consider when thinking about pricing is marginal costs. If your providers already have—even without your marketplace being involved in the equation—very thin profit margins, you cannot expect to take a large chunk of it. A good example is OpenTable, a table booking service with restaurants as providers. Out of each order, most of the money goes towards the salaries of the restaurant personnel, the rent of the restaurant space, the raw ingredients of the meal, and other such costs. The restaurant business is very competitive, so profit margins are very thin. There's not much room for OpenTable to operate in. The same goes for Etsy: the seller needs to buy the material, manufacture the item, and ship it to the buyer. There are lots of sellers out there, so competition is fierce, and profit margins are low.

Meanwhile, the stock photo market is very different, as are digital goods markets in general. Once you've produced a digital product, you can sell it an unlimited number of times for no extra cost. 30% of the sale price is pure profit for the photographer every time they make a sale.

If your marketplace sells different types of products that have great variety in their marginal costs, you might want to consider different commission rates for different product categories. Typical examples of well-known marketplaces that do this are eBay and Amazon. Amazon's fees range from 6% to 45% based on the category of the product.

Competition

Another factor to consider are the different channels through which your providers currently distribute their products or services. Are you their only channel? This might be the case if you manage to find a narrow enough niche that nobody else is catering to (yet). With a monopoly on a niche, you will likely be able to charge more for operating the marketplace. This is another good reason to have a narrow focus, especially in the beginning.

However, a more likely scenario is that other channels exist, and you need to create a competitive offering. Restaurants had customers coming in through various channels when OpenTable started—some of which cost the restaurants nothing!—so the table-booking service needed to have extremely competitive pricing.

Etsy faced a similar situation when it started: many of its sellers were already selling on Amazon or eBay. By setting its fees to only 50% of what its competitors were charging, Etsy positioned itself as an attractive option for sellers. While Etsy likes to claim that it's better than the alternatives in many other ways as well, the pricing strategy definitely helped it carve market share from big competitors—especially in the early days. Etsy has always stressed that it can only succeed if its sellers succeed with their businesses, and a low take rate communicates this viewpoint effectively.

While Etsy's fees are currently quite low, it is facing a lot of pressure. Etsy is a public company, and its shareholders are demanding higher profits, creating pressure to increase commission rates. There might still be an opportunity for competition to take on Etsy. By focusing on a smaller segment, crafting a good value proposition for your providers, and charging lower fees, you might well be able to disrupt Etsy. As Jeff Bezos, the founder of Amazon, famously said: "Your margin is my opportunity."

A great example of how lower pricing can be used to disrupt a market leader is how TaoBao beat eBay in China[25]. If you are competing with a market leader like eBay and Etsy by trying to attract their providers to your platform, you either need to provide more value for your customers and providers (see chapter four), or charge lower fees.

Photographers don't have good alternatives to the large stock photo sites if they want to sell their photographs to large masses. This is why the sites can charge large commissions. Selling photos through a physical retail shop or their own online store are much less effective. However, Shutterstock and other stock photo sites (such as Getty Images, which charges an even higher commission of 80%) are facing tough competition as the cost of building a marketplace business is going down, and new competition is emerging. As we discussed in the previous chapter, Stocksy, the stock photo site owned by the photographers themselves, has been acquiring photographers from bigger competitors in part thanks to its lower fee. There is plenty of opportunity for newcomers in the fat margins of big players.

Network effect

A factor that is closely related to the number of distribution channels is the network effect. A marketplace benefits from the network effect if having more

---

25   www.sharetribe.com/booklinks, #26

providers makes the marketplace more valuable for customers, and vice versa. This is an important reason why stock photo sites have been able to keep their commissions high. A stock photo site becomes infinitely more useful to a customer when its selection increases, especially since each offering on the site is unique. Also, since stock photos are generally needed for very specific topics, customers will flock to the platforms with the widest selection.

On the surface, it might seem that all marketplaces benefit from the network effect. To some extent, this is true. However, especially in the field of local and non-unique services, there can be a cap to this benefit. A good example is on-demand ridesharing, where Lyft has been able to successfully carve market share from Uber, a much bigger and better-funded competitor. As Lyft's CEO John Zimmer explains: "Once you hit three minute pickup times, there's no benefit to having more people on the network." [26]

In the same article, W. Brian Arthur, a theoretician behind network effects, notes that if all the provided services on a marketplace are (nearly) identical, network effects may not be so advantageous. If the marketplace can always meet the needs of a customer with a given set of providers, there's no additional benefit in increasing the number of providers. Venture Capitalist and marketplace specialist James Currier calls this phenomenon an asymptotic network effect[27].

In general, the stronger the benefit from the network effect, the higher your commission can be—as long as your network is big enough. The closer you are to having perfect competition, the less benefit you get from the network.

Provider differentiation

In the real world, most marketplaces are far from perfect competition. There are often various types of providers: some are professionals with multiple daily transactions, while others might only make a sale once or twice

26   www.sharetribe.com/booklinks, #27
27   www.sharetribe.com/booklinks, #28

a year. This poses an interesting pricing question: should you have the same pricing for all providers?

Different marketplaces have taken different strategies for this. eBay offers benefits to people who sell a lot: while the base fee is not lower, *power sellers* enjoy cheaper shipping, unpaid item protection, and promotional offers. Airbnb offers its *superhosts* perks like travel coupons and priority support. The reasoning behind these programs is clearly to encourage people to sell more, and to retain the most successful providers on the platform.

Etsy has taken a different strategy. It offers paid premium services such as direct checkout, shipping labels and promoted listings. These services are specifically targeted towards the platform's premium sellers. Marketplace specialist Boris Wertz calls this the freemium model for marketplace pricing. Wertz explains the rationale:

– *By relying less on monetizing the smaller sellers, the platform ensures that these small sellers can afford to stay on the platform and contribute their crafty and unique inventory that Etsy buyers want. Etsy then takes a higher rate from the big sellers that can most afford it due to their scale[28].*

Bill Gurley mentions that Booking.com used the same approach. It first took over the market with low pricing, but then started offering paid promotion services that increased take rates. Gurley notes: "When prices go up due to bidding and competition, the suppliers blame their competition, not the platform."

Transaction size and volume

Pricing is all about psychology. The one figure your providers really care about is the amount of money you're extracting from each transaction. If they perceive it to be high, they will become suspicious.

---

28   www.sharetribe.com/booklinks, #29

Providers' suspicion does not necessarily directly correlate with your commission percentage. The bigger the total size of a transaction, the smaller the expected percentage. In general, people perceive the marketplace to provide a certain amount of value by facilitating a transaction. Fiverr charges a 20% commission, but since a typical transaction size is only $5, it doesn't sound that big: it's only $1 per transaction, after all.

If transaction sizes vary a lot in your marketplace, you need to consider whether having the same fee for all transactions makes sense or not. Airbnb's rates for guests vary from 12 to 20 percent based on the size of the total transaction. The higher the total sum, the lower the commission. This way Airbnb encourages customers to make bigger purchases.

As a marketplace founder, you need to build a sustainable business model by evaluating your market closely: how many potential transactions can you expect to get in a month, and what do you expect the total transaction size to be? You can use this handy calculator[29] to find the optimal price point for your marketplace.

If you feel that your market is huge, you will probably have more competition. This also means that you will likely need to keep your pricing low. This does not necessarily mean low profits, however. Gurley quotes the famous business educator Peter Drucker:

– *High profit margins do not equal maximum profits. Total profit is profit margin multiplied by turnover. Maximum profit is thus obtained by the profit margin that yields the largest total profit flow.*

Quality vs quantity

As you learned from the previous chapter, the key to keeping transactions in your platform is to provide as much value as possible for both sides of your marketplace. The amount of value provided naturally correlates strongly with your pricing. If you provide more value, the perceived quality of your offering

---

29   www.sharetribe.com/booklinks, #30

is higher, which justifies higher prices. The better you are at communicating the high quality of your offering to your customers, the easier it is to charge more.

A good example of how to provide additional value—and thus increase quality—is with insurance for rental marketplaces. If the marketplace is insuring the rented item, it is easy for both the provider and the customer to accept the cost related to the transaction. They can clearly see what they are getting for the fee.

Vetting providers is another common way to enhance quality. While some marketplaces let anyone become a provider, others curate the onboarding carefully, hand-picking each provider and possibly conducting a background check, or giving the customers the tools to do so. This is especially important in quality-intensive marketplaces such as dog boarding, babysitting, or taking care of the elderly. Stocksy is using the vetting strategy effectively[30] to disrupt the stock photo market.

You need to decide whether you want to focus on quantity—getting as many providers as possible to increase your selection—or quality—curating your selection carefully. In the latter case, your pricing should likely be higher to communicate the value you provide, whereas in the former case you need to keep your margins low to get as many people on board as possible. Sometimes both of these strategies can be applied to the same market.

Who pays the bill?

Since marketplaces have two sides—the customer and the provider—an important consideration is which party pays the bill. In practice, both mean the same thing: the money is split between you and your provider. However, for psychological reasons, how you communicate this can make a big difference.

An important factor is whether your marketplace is supply-constrained or demand-constrained. As marketplace expert Jeff Jordan (previously CEO of

---

30   www.sharetribe.com/booklinks, #31

OpenTable and GM of eBay) notes[31], many traditional marketplaces like eBay and OpenTable are demand-constrained: once there are enough customers, the providers will flock to the marketplace. On the other hand, sharing economy marketplaces like Airbnb are an example of supply-constrained marketplaces, especially in the beginning: it was tricky to convince people to rent their houses out to strangers, so the limiting factor was supply.

As Bill Gurley states, "you want to build a platform that has the least amount of friction for both product and pricing. High rakes are a form of friction". In general, you want to lower the friction for the side that you are constrained with. That is why eBay and OpenTable charge the providers, but Airbnb places most of the fees on the guests.

In the classical Harvard Business Review article on marketplace dynamics, "Strategies for Two-Sided Markets"[32], the authors Thomas R. Eisenmann, Geoffrey G. Parker and Marshall W. Van Alstyne argue that in some cases, it even makes sense for the platform to subsidize the most price-sensitive side to reduce friction and capture market share. This tactic has recently been employed by Uber, which slashed its pricing due to increased competition, and tried to prevent the backlash from drivers by paying them more than they "earned"[33]. Naturally, this strategy requires a lot of capital to work.

Summary

As we've seen, a number of factors affect the pricing decision. As a simple framework, we present the following: start from 10%, and then look into how your marketplace is positioned in terms of the seven factors mentioned in this chapter (marginal costs, distribution channels, network effect, provider differentiation, transaction size and volume, quality vs quantity, and who pays the bill). Based on that analysis, adjust the percentage.

---

31   www.sharetribe.com/booklinks, #32
32   www.sharetribe.com/booklinks, #33
33   www.sharetribe.com/booklinks, #34

In general, you should take as little as you need to remain sustainable. As Bill Gurley states:

– *High rakes are a form of friction precisely because your rake becomes part of the landed price for the consumer. If you charge an excessive rake, the pricing of items in your marketplace are now unnaturally high (relative to anything outside your marketplace). In order for your platform to be the 'definitive' place to transact, you want industry-leading pricing—which is impossible if your rake is the de facto cause of excessive pricing. High rakes also create a natural impetus for suppliers to look elsewhere, which endangers sustainability.*[34]

Remember that it's ok to change pricing, and you probably should iterate on it as you go. However, it's always difficult to raise prices, so starting off with a higher price and then reducing it if needed is probably the better strategy. If you wish to get more supply in the beginning by offering cheaper pricing—which is often a good idea—you should consider offering time-based discounts ("First 6 months with 50% discount on fees!"). It is important to clearly communicate that pricing will return to normal levels after the initial discount period.

---

34   www.sharetribe.com/booklinks, #24

6

How to validate your idea before building the platform

You have now crystallized your idea and chosen a viable business model for it. At this stage, you are likely eager to start building your online platform and launch it as soon as possible. Intuitively, this makes a lot of sense: as was mentioned in the second chapter, the final validation of your business will happen only after you have launched the platform and have people using it.

However, there are a number of things you can—and should—do before writing the first line of code, hiring anyone to build the platform or even using a turnkey solution like Sharetribe to launch it. It is possible to prevalidate many assumptions about your idea and business model without having a platform at all. In this chapter, we will go over why and how you should do it.

Why you need to validate your idea

The first startup project Cristóbal got involved with—back in 2006—was a music quiz platform. The team worked really hard on the platform. The founders had some money to invest, so they hired a skilled CTO to develop it. Cristóbal only spent a year with the team, but the others kept at it for almost four years. A lot of time was spent on strategy and coding. They attended networking events and pitched to potential investors.

Unfortunately, their users were not engaging with the product in the way that they hoped. When they realized the platform wasn't working, it was too late to pivot. They had spent too much time and money building the wrong things. The project failed.

After taking some time off, Cristóbal got excited by another platform idea in 2009. He taught himself Drupal to develop a marketplace platform where users could help each other out in various ways. He spent thousands of hours learning how to build a platform, and did research on various case studies like Couchsurfing and Freecycle. He spent two years working on the project, but finally learned that his product did not really solve a real problem for his users. In the process, he managed to waste a lot of time.

At the same time, Juho was helping several Finnish universities, companies and associations launch their own internal community marketplaces. He found that while many organizations were interested in the idea, the platforms generally failed to get traction. In most cases, the organizations wanted to make their employee, student or member community more connected and sustainable, and thought creating a marketplace would be a good way to achieve that. What they failed to do was ask their members beforehand whether such a platform was actually something they really needed.

Since having these experiences, we have both studied many similar cases from other marketplace entrepreneurs. Adam Berk, the founder of an early neighborhood sharing platform *neigh*borrow*, describes how their platform failed due to not validating their core assumptions. Berk writes:

– *We spent far too much time building and stressing over parts of the site that were like 10 assumptions deep. There were 50 ways we could have made money but we had zero ways of actually making money. For a long time, we spun our wheels trying to figure out the disconnect. Maybe we should raise more money. Or we just needed more media coverage, now that we've nailed that last A/B test. Perhaps it was our design, which didn't pop. No, wait, it might be that we were too focused and should expand beyond bikes and drills.*

– Based on these experiences and stories from others, we have come to the conclusion that not validating your business idea and strategy is the worst mistake that budding marketplace entrepreneurs make today.[35]

As we mentioned in the first chapter of this book, many marketplace startup teams waste time and money developing "desert platforms"—platforms which are well built but fail to generate traction. This usually happens due to not validating the business idea and strategy.

We have seen many teams waste their time arguing about the colour of their logo when they really should be talking to their potential users to better understand their real problems.

Entrepreneurs tend to fall in love with their own ideas. And when they do, they easily ignore feedback from users—especially if it conflicts with their original idea. Many fall victim to the "entrepreneur illusion": if we only work hard, we will eventually succeed. Don't do that. If the idea is no good, no amount of hard work will make it better. As agile and lean coach Henrik Kniberg puts it[36], instead of maximizing output, you should maximize value. He illustrates this with the following picture.

35   www.sharetribe.com/booklinks, #35
36   www.sharetribe.com/booklinks, #36

Maximize Value, not Output

Henrik Kniberg

Image courtesy of Henrik Kniberg, from presentation Spotify – the unproject culture[37]

What you should validate

As venture capitalist Marc Andreessen puts it, the only thing that matters in the beginning is finding product/market fit[38]. Product/market fit means being in a good market with a product that can satisfy the demand in that market.

Startup guru Steve Blank breaks this down further[39]. The first step is *customer discovery*, or achieving *problem/solution fit*. By the end of the customer discovery stage, you should have an idea of what kind of an *MVP* (*Minimum Viable Product*—or, in your case, *Minimum Viable Platform*) you need to build. Only after you reach problem/solution fit is it time to build the MVP. We'll discuss building the MVP in the next chapter. In this chapter we are going to focus on getting to problem/solution fit.

---

37   www.sharetribe.com/booklinks, #36
38   www.sharetribe.com/booklinks, #37
39   www.sharetribe.com/booklinks, #38

To achieve problem/solution fit, the first thing to do is to write down your assumptions. Every business idea begins from a set of hypotheses from the founders, and your goal should be to understand what they are and how to validate them as quickly as possible.

Plenty of handy tools for building the set of assumptions in a systematic way exist. Steve Blank recommends starting with the Business Model Canvas (BMC)[40]. Using the canvas, you map out the different aspects of your business: your value propositions, your customer segments, your distribution channels, your revenue streams, and so on. You will likely have assumptions in all of these areas that need to be validated. During the validation process, you will most likely realize that some of these assumptions are wrong. The sooner these are discovered, the better—you don't want to waste resources building something based on incorrect assumptions.

Marketplace business models are quite specific to marketplaces, so sometimes it can be tricky to adapt BMC to them. When Cristóbal and others members of the platform design toolkit[41] team are advising marketplaces businesses, they use a set of canvases designed specifically for building multi-sided platforms by platform expert Simone Cicero. One of the tools is the Platform Design Canvas, a version of the BMC built specifically with marketplaces and other platforms in mind.

Lots of literature has been written on the topic of validating business models. If you only choose to read one book, we recommend *The Lean Startup*, an iconic work by Eric Ries. Lean Startup and the concepts pioneered by Ries have since grown into a movement that has helped thousands of entrepreneurs. We would have both certainly saved lots of time and money had we known of these methods when we started our startup journey. This book spurred an entire movement of applying "lean" manufacturing principles to building businesses. This movement has also inspired the name of the book you're reading.

---

40   www.sharetribe.com/booklinks, #39
41   www.sharetribe.com/booklinks, #40

If you are a bootstrapping entrepreneur with little money to spend, you will also enjoy Ash Maurya's book *Running Lean* as a follow-up to The Lean Startup. Maurya offers many practical tools and step-by-step instructions for entrepreneurs who are building internet companies—things like how to find potential users to interview before launching, how to conduct the interviews, and how to analyze the data gathered in them and draw conclusions from them.

How to validate your assumptions

Now that you know what needs to be validated, it is time to take a very concrete example and look at how to actually validate the assumptions in practice.

When we work with marketplace entrepreneurs, we like to start the validation process by applying the Customer-Problem-Solution Hypothesis from "The Entrepreneur's guide to Customer Development"[42]. It provides some questions that help you get started with the validation process:

- What problem(s) are you trying to solve?
- Who has the problem?
- How is this person dealing with the problem now?
- How are you planning to solve the problem?
- Why is your solution better?

List the assumptions

Let's say you are planning to build a marketplace for personal trainer services. You got the idea based on your personal problems as an existing customer of personal training services. You first list the assumptions from a customer's point of view, based on your own experiences.

- Searching for a personal trainer using Google is not convenient: it takes time to go through a list of different websites.

---

42   www.sharetribe.com/booklinks, #41

- Discovering the best personal trainers in a certain location is difficult. There is no easy way to compare local providers and find the one that best suits you.
- Finding a free time slot and paying for the service is complicated since every provider has their own reservation and payment system.

Marketplaces always have two sides, and as we've discussed in chapter two, you need to solve a problem for both sides. In other words, you also need to consider the viewpoint of personal trainers (the providers). While you are not a personal trainer yourself, you come up with several assumptions about their problems:

- Many providers don't have enough customers because they do not know how to promote themselves online. They might not even have a personal website, and if they do, the quality is lackluster, which hurts their brand.
- The personal trainer market is not as big as it could be because finding and booking a trainer is such a hurdle. If it were easier, more people would use the services of personal trainers, and they would all have more customers.
- Personal trainers do not have sufficient tools for managing their booking schedules and invoicing their customers. Streamlining this process would bring value to them.
- While most personal trainers have traditionally been averse to using online tools, the situation is changing and they are now more willing to move to the digital age.

Based on these problem assumptions, you come up with assumptions for value propositions, distribution channels, and revenue streams. You break them down as follows:

- Value proposition for customers: Easy to use and unified search experience that aggregates lots of providers in one place, allowing for easy comparison based on trainers' offerings and the number of reviews they've received, along with an easy way to book a suitable time slot and pay for it.

- Value proposition for providers: An easy way to set up their own online presence, more leads, and handy tools for managing bookings and invoicing.
- Distribution channel for customers: Since many people are already searching for personal trainer services, they find your site through search engines once you get the first position for certain keyword searches.
- Distribution channel for providers: At first, you build supply by contacting the providers directly and convincing them to join. Later on, growth will come through word of mouth.
- Revenue stream from customers: Your site is free to use for customers.
- Revenue stream from providers: You plan on making money by using the most popular revenue stream for modern marketplaces: charging a commission from each booking from the providers.

Interview your users

That's quite a list of assumptions! Now it's time to start validating them. That means getting out of the building and interviewing both your potential providers (personal trainers) and customers (people who already use or have used personal training services). You should try to find at least 10 people from both groups for a big enough sample. *Running Lean* provides useful interview templates for this stage. You can use their validation board[43] to track your progress.

Some example questions for potential customers:

- How do you currently find personal trainer services?
- How often do you search for new personal trainer services?

---

43   www.sharetribe.com/booklinks, #42

- How do you know which personal trainer services would be the best for you?
- Do you compare different providers somehow?
- Is it easy to book a personal trainer?
- Is it easy to pay for the personal training services?

Some example questions for potential providers:

- Could you take in more customers than you currently have?
- How do your customers currently find you?
- How do you currently manage customers' bookings?
- How do you invoice your customers?
- Do you have a web presence? If not, why?

It is important that you do not lead the interviewees too much in order to get the answers you want. Instead, you should ask them relatively open-ended questions, listen carefully to what they say, and react to their answers with more questions. At least some of your assumptions will most likely be wrong; finding these should be your focus. You are not selling anything yet, so do not talk about the benefits of your solution at the beginning of the interview. Instead, focus on the problem. It's also usually easier to get people to agree to an interview instead of a sales meeting.

If you end up discovering that your assumptions seem to hold true, you can move on to talking about your proposed solution and gauge their reaction to it. When you are talking to the people who you plan on charging (the providers, in this case), remember to also ask whether they would be willing to pay the price you plan on asking (10% of the total booking size, for example). If, on the other hand, you notice that your problem assumptions are wrong, it is better to skip describing your solution and focus on finding out whether there is another problem you could solve for the interviewees instead.

Conducting these interviews yourself is crucial. You need to get to really know your potential users and understand their real problems, which might be completely different from what you were expecting them to be.

For instance, you might learn that the personal trainers are already using a good tool for booking and invoicing, and that their biggest problem is getting more leads. This means that you might need to shift your revenue stream plan: the personal trainers will likely not want to pay for each transaction if you are not able to offer them a big enough improvement for their invoicing process. Instead, you might want to charge per lead, or charge the providers a subscription fee.

On the customer side, you might notice that while customers feel that comparing providers is difficult, it is an activity they only engage in once every two years. Since a single customer will not engage in many transactions, it means you need to attract a large mass of customers for your business model to work. As Bill Gurley notes in his classic article "All Markets Are Not Created Equal":

– *Many failed marketplaces attack purchasing cycles that are simply way too infrequent, which makes it much more difficult to build brand awareness and word-of-mouth customer growth.*[44]

Based on the data, you might notice that some people are more responsive towards your idea than others. After enough interviews, you start to notice certain patterns. Maybe younger people like the idea more? Or perhaps a very specific customer demographic (like wealthy stay-at-home moms between 30 and 50) has way more potential than other segments. After making such a discovery, you can focus on just the customers in this specific segment and how to solve their problems. Remember: it's much better to initially make a product a small number of users love than a product that a large number of users like.

Study search data

Some assumptions are more difficult to validate with interviews. For instance, you might base your business model on the assumption that there

---

44   www.sharetribe.com/booklinks, #43

are 50,000 potential customers in a city with 1 million people, and they will find you mainly through search engines. How do you validate this assumption?

Luckily, there's a method for this type of validation too: you can study what people are searching for online. For instance, with tools like Semrush, you can study how often a certain keyword is searched.

After reading the previous chapters of this book, you know the importance of focus, especially in the early days. Since personal training services are local, you will likely want to focus on only one city in the beginning.

Let's say you live in Dallas, Texas and want to start from your home turf (which is probably a good idea). You can now check how many people search for "personal trainer Dallas" every month. If you can get everyone who makes this search sign up for your site, is it enough to justify your business model? More realistically, even if you manage to get your site as the first search result (which can be very difficult), only 5-10% of those people will likely sign up. Is that still enough?

You should also try searching for this term on Google yourself to see what you are up against. Who are your biggest competitors? Are there already lots of ads for your ideal keyword? If there are, you will likely need to work (or pay) more to reach the top position—not to mention offering more value to your users than your competition.

Summary

In this chapter, we have gone over why marketplace idea validation is important. Not validating assumptions can end up being extremely expensive, both in terms of time and money.

Before building anything, you should write down all assumptions related to your problem, value proposition, business model and distribution channels, and validate them using customer interviews and search data. It is quite likely that some of your initial assumptions were invalidated. On the other hand, you now have previously unknown information that opens up new opportunities.

After going through this process, you should have a relatively good idea of your users' real problems and possible solutions. You should be much closer to problem/solution fit.

The next step is to start building the Minimum Viable Platform (MVP): the smallest possible solution that solves your users' problem in a way that is better than the existing solutions out there. With the MVP, you can start searching for product/market fit.

In the next four chapters, we are going to focus on building the MVP.

7

How to build a Minimum Viable Platform

Once you have gone through the initial process of customer discovery, you should have a relatively good idea of what your users' real problems are and how to solve them. In other words, you should be close to problem/solution fit. The next step is achieving product/market fit—finding a big enough market with a product that can satisfy that market.

To find product/market fit, you need to build a minimum viable product (MVP)[45]: a minimal solution that solves the core problem of your users better than other existing solutions. The product is then released to your users to kick off the learning process.

In this chapter, we focus on how to build your MVP.

What is a Minimum Viable Product?

The term Minimum Viable Product was popularised by startup gurus Eric Ries and Steve Blank, and it's at the core of the lean startup philosophy. Blank refers to the approach of a MVP as *"selling the vision and delivering the minimum feature set to visionaries, not everyone."*

---

[45]   www.sharetribe.com/booklinks, #44

It is important to define who your early adopters are—the people most eager to try out your solution and give feedback—and then develop the core feature set (and nothing more) that allows you to solve their needs. After they start using your product, these early adopters will provide you with invaluable information about how to improve the product. You should continuously listen to their input, make small improvements based on the feedback, deliver these improvements to the users and talk to them again to see if the issues were solved. As Eric Ries puts it:

– *The minimum viable product is that version of a new product which allows a team to collect the maximum amount of validated learning about customers with the least effort.*

The concept of an MVP is closely related to the field of agile software development. The point of agility is to build, deliver and learn quickly. Agile and lean coach Henrik Kniberg illustrates the benefits of the agile approach versus the traditional waterfall-style product development with the following picture.

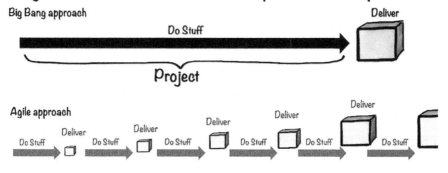

Image courtesy of Henrik Kniberg, from presentation Spotify – the unproject culture[46]

---

46   www.sharetribe.com/booklinks, #36

Even when building an MVP, you need to know what to build. Many startups fail because they start building an MVP without proper pre-validation (see previous chapter), and end up with products that nobody use. For true learning to happen, even the first version of your MVP needs to be good enough to really solve an identified problem. The following picture from Henrik Kniberg illustrates how to approach building an MVP, and how not to do it.

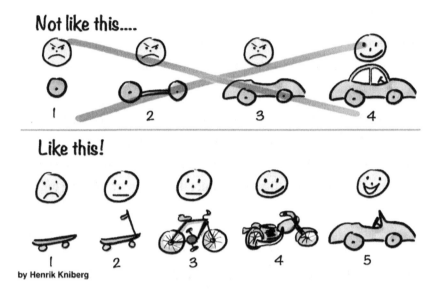

Image courtesy of Henrik Kniberg, from presentation Spotify – the unproject culture

In some cases, building a working solution is a complex process that requires lots of work. Typical examples include physical products or more advanced software solutions. In these cases, the MVP can be a non-functional prototype that validates demand before getting the actual product in the hands of customers.

For example, you might make a video that explains how the product works and combine it with a call to action to purchase the product or sign up. Pebble did this with their successful smartwatch Kickstarter campaign, and file storage service Dropbox did it with their product video and mailing list[47].

However, if it is possible to get a working prototype in the hands of customers with relatively little effort, that is definitely the recommended approach. The launch story of Buffer, a social media automation tool, is a great case study on this. They went from idea to paying customers in 7 weeks[48].

Is viable enough?

A common mistake entrepreneurs make is to assume that the MVP can be really buggy or ugly. This is not the case. While the MVP does not necessarily need to be polished to perfection, it needs to contain a set of required features—ones that work properly and delight the user. If your software is broken or looks unfinished, it will give a very bad first impression and deter users. The following illustration by user experience designer Jussi Pasanen exemplifies how you should approach the MVP.

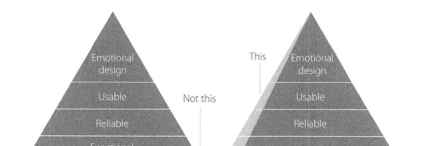

Minimum Viable Product: Build a slice across, instead of one layer at a time. Diagram courtesy of Jussi Pasanen, with acknowledgements to Aarron Walter, Ben Tollady, Ben Rowe, Lexi Thorn and Senthil Kugalur.

---

47   www.sharetribe.com/booklinks, #45
48   www.sharetribe.com/booklinks, #46

Alex Iskold, Managing Director at Techstars in NYC, notes[49] how the emphasis of startups that are building their MVPs is too often on the word minimum. Founders following the lean startup principles tend to misinterpret the concept of MVP and launch products that are too raw and simple. This results in nobody using them, and entrepreneurs concluding that their entire idea is bad when the MVP just was not quite there yet. Do not fall into this trap.

Instead of focusing on just being minimum or viable, we like to encourage budding marketplace entrepreneurs to design MVPs that aim to delight their early adopter users. This approach is called building a Minimum Lovable Product (MLP), a term coined by the great team behind the The Happy Startup School[50].

The MLP is "the version of a new product that brings back the maximum amount of love from your early tribe members with the least effort." We highly recommend checking out their "10 tips to go from viable to lovable"[51].

Marketing expert Rand Fishkin also talks about the same issue. He encourages entrepreneurs to "not deliver mediocrity but put in the time and effort required to be remarkable"[52], and building an exceptional viable product before releasing it.

Minimum Viable Platform

We have been talking about Minimum Viable Products in general, and are now going to focus specifically on marketplaces. In the case of a marketplace business, an MVP means a Minimum Viable Platform. This term was coined by marketplace expert Sangeet Paul Choudary, who discusses how a platform should start by providing a single interaction between its two sides[53].

There is no going around it: when building a marketplace business, you can only validate product/market fit by launching a platform and getting your

---

49   www.sharetribe.com/booklinks, #47
50   http://www.thehappystartupschool.com/
51   www.sharetribe.com/booklinks, #48
52   www.sharetribe.com/booklinks, #49
53   www.sharetribe.com/booklinks, #50

users to transact on it. In this particular field, a crowdfunding campaign or a video is not enough—as we've learned, many people will say they love your idea and may even sign up, but the real test is whether they actually use your platform to interact with other users. Only then will you know that you are truly providing value.

Let us go back to the example of building a marketplace for personal trainers services that we used in the previous chapter. You have interviewed some potential users and identified the most promising customer segment. The main assumptions from both the customers' and providers' point of view were validated. You now have a clear value proposition for both sides of your marketplace, and based on the interviews (and perhaps other experiments) you are quite sure it is a big enough problem to solve.

You write down your value propositions as follows:

- Value proposition for customers (wealthy stay-at-home moms between 35 and 55): Easy to use and unified search experience that aggregates many personal trainers into one place, allows comparisons based on offerings and the number of reviews they have received, and makes it easy to book a suitable time slot and pay for it.
- Value proposition for providers (personal trainers): An easy way to set up their own online presence, generate more leads, and provides handy tools for managing bookings and invoicing.

Now you are ready to build a minimum viable solution that offers this value proposition. The only true validation of your idea is if, what Steve Blank calls, *earlyvangelists54* (*early adopters + internal evangelists*) start booking personal training services through your solution. This is your goal for this stage.

---

54   www.sharetribe.com/booklinks, #51

Consider starting with a concierge MVP

You might be wondering whether you need a lot of money at this point. After all, you need to build a platform to validate your concept, and building software is costly. Thankfully, you might be able to get your first bookings without building any custom software.

The purpose of your marketplace is to match supply and demand. Eventually, you will want to automate the matchmaking with software, but in the beginning, you can play the role of the matchmaking software yourself. This approach is called the concierge MVP[55].

In the case of the personal trainer marketplace, you could start by convincing 10 trainers to offer their services through your platform. The next step is to create a simple landing page—using a tool like Unbounce, Instapage, or Strikingly that require no coding—with a list of the personal trainers, descriptions of their services and prices. You would also create a simple booking form (with a free tool like Typeform or Google Forms) that would simply ask for the customer's email address, the trainer they want to book from, and the desired time.

Each booking email would land in your inbox. You would then communicate with the trainer and the customer to arrange a suitable date, and would ask the customer to confirm the booking with a payment. A tool like PayPal's payment pages can be used to accept the incoming payments, after which you can transfer the payment (minus your commission fee) to the trainer.

After each successful booking, you would email the customer and ask them to rate the provider. You would then manually add the review to your landing page.

Whenever someone makes a booking request, you can add their email address to a mailing list tool like MailChimp. Whenever you add new personal trainers to the system or have special offers from existing providers, you can email all the people on your list.

---

55   www.sharetribe.com/booklinks, #52

The solution described above offers your basic value proposition to both sides of your marketplace. This approach is exactly what Airbnb initially started with, and it worked well for them. As Jared Friedman (partner at Y Combinator) explained at the RiseUp Summit 2015:

> – *The first version of Airbnb was a WordPress blog where they just put down a list of apartments you can rent. They didn't even write any code. In order to rent you would just leave a comment on the blog saying you want to stay there. It was super ghetto! But in launching that, they were able to see what people want.*[56]

Airbnb's current design and features were built only after their basic concept was thoroughly validated.

You can go even simpler than a landing page. Ryan Hoover talks about email-first startups[57], which don't necessarily even have a landing page, but instead just an email address where the users can post their needs.

By using the concierge MVP approach, you can validate (or invalidate) many of your core assumptions without spending much time or money. Naturally, the approach doesn't scale beyond the initial transactions, but that's ok. As Paul Graham, founder of Y-Combinator, famously advised Airbnb founders: in the beginning you specifically should do things that don't scale[58].

When to start building your own software

It is possible that the concierge MVP approach does not make for a good enough Minimum Lovable Platform in your specific case. The web has evolved lot since the days Airbnb got started. People are now more used to searching, making bookings and paying online, and are used to stellar user experiences. In other words, the bar is a lot higher. As Rand Fishkin says, it is not enough

---

56   www.sharetribe.com/booklinks, #53
57   www.sharetribe.com/booklinks, #54
58   www.sharetribe.com/booklinks, #55

to deliver something that works—you need to deliver something exceptional from the beginning.

You might already have competitors who do things the manual way, so your unique value proposition could be based on automating the matchmaking in a new way—perhaps you're the first platform in your industry that allows the entire booking and payment process to happen online in seconds instead of requiring back and forth via email and phone. In this case, the only way to validate your value proposition is to build the software that does this right from the beginning. You still want to keep the amount of custom software you build to a minimum, but the core software elements need to be there.

Furthermore, even if the manual-first approach works for you in the beginning, it's important to remember that as soon as you have validated the initial value proposition, you need to move on to validate your business model. This is where many marketplaces go wrong: they fail to get to *unit economics*— direct costs and revenues related to their business model—that would lead to a profitable business.

Imagine you're building a startup for home cleaners. On average, you spend $15 to get a new customer to make a purchase (when combining advertising costs, manual support for the customer, and so on). The average purchase size is $50, and your commission is 20%, which amounts to $10. This means that you're losing $5 for every transaction on your site. This is what has been the demise of many venture-backed marketplaces: they grew very fast until they suddenly went bankrupt since their model was based on "selling dollar bills for 90 cents".

In the concierge approach, your business model is not yet scalable. You might already be making money, but you're spending a lot more than you're making on each transaction, if for nothing else then at least because of the time you spend. To validate your ability to actually make a profit, you will need software. Next we'll discuss how to approach building it.

How to build the software for your platform

The approach you should take depends on three main factors: your budget, whether you are a programmer (or have programmers on your team), and how quickly you need to go to market.

If you're not technical and have a limited budget, you have two options. One of them is to find a technical co-founder and have them build the platform for "free" (in exchange for equity). However, this is easier said than done. As Buffer CEO Joel Gascoigne notes: *"I believe you'll struggle to find a great technical co-founder if all you have is your idea."*[59] What's more, you should be extremely picky about who to start a business with—it's a long-term partnership that can make or break your business, so you don't want to make the choice too hastily. If you are going to wait until you find a suitable person, you might need to wait for a long time. And as we have discussed, it is vital to launch your idea as early as possible.

The other option is to use a software-as-a-service marketplace solution, like Sharetribe or Arcadier. Many such solutions allow you to build a basic platform without technical skills. The starting price can be less than $100 per month. The downside of using such software is that you're limited to their current feature set, and some functionality you need for your platform might be missing. However, in many cases, this approach can still provide a good enough starting point, and will get you to a place where you are able to invest more resources into custom development—acquiring funding and finding a technical co-founder become easier once you can show some traction.

If you have a higher budget, you can consider hiring a freelancer or an agency to build the platform for you. If you're a small startup, this is often still cheaper than committing to hiring someone full-time. However, you should be extremely careful with this approach as it's easy to waste a lot of time and money with it. As Gascoigne points out, your goals and the goals of the freelancer are often misaligned. As a marketplace founder, you want to

---

59   www.sharetribe.com/booklinks, #56

constantly adapt your platform and iterate, and build only the minimal feature set required. Meanwhile, a freelancer would prefer a project with clear fixed scope, and ideally a large amount of features defined upfront.

This problem goes away if you are technical yourself or have programmers on your team. However, it can still take a surprisingly long time to build a fully functional marketplace from scratch.

To avoid spending lots of time or money, it often makes sense to consider a hybrid solution where you use an existing marketplace software solution as a basis, and build the customizations you need on top of it (or get them built by a freelancer). This way you can limit the scope of the customization project, decrease the time to market, and still get the flexibility you need.

How to choose the right marketplace software

There are dozens of marketplace software solutions out there, and we encounter new solutions monthly. Doing a full comparison is not possible within the scope of this book. Furthermore, any such analysis would be biased since Juho's company Sharetribe offers one such solution.

Instead, what we can do is to offer you the tools for comparing the different software vendors yourself and choosing the one that fits your particular concept best. These are the things you should consider when choosing a marketplace software vendor.

What is the focus of the software?

There is no software solution that handles all different types of marketplace ideas perfectly. The more focused the marketplace software is to your specific industry, the more likely it is to be a good choice for you.

Multiple different dimensions affect the choice of software:

- Is your marketplace about selling products or services?
- If it's about products, are they physical or digital?
- Is it consumer-to-consumer (C2C), business-to-consumer (B2C), or business-to-business (B2B)?

- Do you want to build a website or a mobile app?

As an example, Sharetribe is a good fit for building C2C marketplaces that deal with rentals or selling pre-owned products, or B2C marketplaces that deal with local services. Meanwhile, Izberg is a good fit for those looking to build an Amazon-style marketplace where retailers sell their products. If you are focusing on digital products, Marketify combined with Easy Digital Downloads might be a good solution for you. If you need an Uber-style ride hailing app, you might want to take a look at LibreTaxi.

How easy it is to extend the software

While an off-the-shelf software solution might be enough for initial validation, sooner or later you will need to build features specific to your concept—your secret sauce that separates you from the competition. Due to the unique nature of these features, your marketplace software vendor most likely doesn't offer them out of the box. Building a new platform from scratch at this point would be extremely painful, so you need to make sure your vendor offers the possibility to extend their platform to avoid being locked in.

If the vendor's software is open source, you're good to go: you can simply take the code, install it to your own server, and customize away. However, this approach also has its downsides. Since marketplace software can be quite complex, it means a steep learning curve for your developers. It might also contain features you don't really need, which can slow down customization work. Finally, it locks into you to using specific technologies instead of allowing your developers to use the language and frameworks they are most comfortable with. Thus, before moving forward with an open source solution, be sure to get an opinion on the customizability of the codebase from a developer.

An alternative to this approach is a model where you access all your marketplace data via an application programming interface (API) provided by a vendor. This allows your developers to fully customize the workflow and user interface of your platform, integrate any third party software, or build mobile apps. At the same time, you benefit from the core marketplace functionality offered by the vendor, like search, payments, messaging, reviews, availability and scheduling, moderation, and analytics tools for the marketplace operator.

Is the vendor's business model aligned with yours?

Entering into a partnership with a marketplace software provider is a major decision. You want to be sure that their interests are aligned with yours. The best way to understand this is to look into how they are making money.

If the vendor is charging a large amount of money up front, before you have launched anything, beware. In such a model, the vendor makes money whether you succeed or not, which means their incentives can be similar to that of freelancers'.

If the revenue model of the vendor is based on your user or transaction volume, you're probably in good hands: they will only make significant money if you do as well, which is a good starting point for a partnership.

What kinds of services does the vendor provide?

Does the vendor offer hosting, server monitoring, automatic software updates and data backups? If you're not technical, you will need all these from them. You also want to make sure they adhere to all security best practices and handle regulatory compliance.

Many vendors offer some kind of a free trial period. You should use this time before committing to a purchase, and test all the aspects of the software thoroughly. During this time, it's also a good idea to be in touch with the vendor's customer support. Based on our experience, you will end up communicating with the customer support of your marketplace vendor a lot as your platform starts growing, so you want to make sure they answer quickly and to the point, and that it's easy for you to make yourself understood.

What references does the vendor have?

Ask them how long they have been in business, how big their team is, their financial situation, how many paying customers they have, and examples of their most successful customers, in general and in your industry. You want to find a vendor that is willing to both share such information openly and demonstrate that they themselves have traction and others have been able to succeed with them.

Measuring the success of your MVP

Once your MVP is ready, you can launch it to your users. We will explore launch strategies in chapter twelve. However, before launching, it is important to define what you want to learn from the launch. Remember that the launch of the MVP is just an experiment, the purpose of which is to provide you with information about whether your assumptions were correct. As Eric Ries notes, if your goal is to simply launch something and see what happens, you'll always succeed in that, but it doesn't necessarily help you validate your assumptions.

The key questions you should answer before launching the MVP are the following:

- What assumptions are you trying to validate in this experiment?
- What data are you collecting through this experiment?
- What determines the success or failure of this experiment?

To answer these questions, you need to define the Key Performance Indicators (KPIs) of your marketplace business. These indicators need to be actionable: if the figures are not what you expected, you need to act on them and change something. We will go deeper into marketplace metrics in chapter 14.

The launch of the MVP is just the beginning of the learning process. After launching, you should be monitoring your KPIs constantly and getting feedback on your users. Based on this learning, you should then continuously improve the MVP, and start the learning cycle all over again.

Summary

A Minimum Viable Product (MVP)—or, in the case of marketplaces, a Minimum Viable Platform—can be defined as the minimal solution that solves your users' core problem better than alternative solutions. With marketplaces, your MVP needs to provide a solution for both sides of the marketplace. You shouldn't focus too much on the word "minimum"—the solution still needs to delight your users. A better term might be a Minimum Lovable Platform instead.

A concierge MVP is often good way to approach building a Minimum Viable Platform. In this model, you manually handle several parts of the product that you will later automate with software.

Sometimes a concierge MVP is not enough, so you need to build custom software. You can either build the software from scratch, use an off-the-shelf marketplace software, or use an existing software product as a base and build the custom features you need on top of it.

If you decide to use an existing marketplace software solution, there are several factors you should consider when choosing the vendor: the focus of the software, how easy it is to extend it, the alignment of the vendor's business model with yours, what kinds of services the vendor provides, and what references they have.

After you have an MVP, you should define your Key Performance Indicators that help you validate your assumptions, and then launch your MVP to your users to see if the assumptions really hold true. Once the MVP is out, you should constantly get feedback on it and improve it based on what you learn.

In this chapter, you've learned how to approach building the very first version of your platform. In the next three chapters, we'll dive into the details of the key building blocks of these platforms.

8

How to communicate your value proposition to your users

Attention span has become shorter. With the rapid growth in the number of online services vying for people's attention, if you do not make an impression on your users within seconds, they will abandon your platform.

When building your marketplace MVP, it is important to consider what kind of first impression it gives to new users, and how it communicates your core value proposition. The unique two-sided nature of marketplaces poses additional communicational challenges: you are catering to two audiences in the same product, the customers and the providers.

Many marketplace entrepreneurs have told us how they struggle to find the right communication strategies. Traditional advertising agencies have not been able to help them due to a lack of understanding of how marketplace businesses work.

As a founder, you should have a crystal clear picture of the value that you provide your users. You need to know who you are targeting and what kind of communication style and aesthetics they appreciate. This chapter will help you figure out the right way to communicate with your users.

Understand your target audience

All too often we meet founders who don't choose the right words to communicate their value proposition to their users. They pitch for 15 minutes without saying a word about the problem they are solving or what the main value proposition is. You need to take the time to simplify your message and prepare a clear pitch with the core elements of your value proposition. If you are not explaining your idea clearly, chances are it won't be understood.

There are several different approaches[60] to crafting your value proposition. It is quite likely that your first choice will not be the best one. Your value proposition sentence is one of the first things you should A/B test as soon as you have enough traffic on your site.

It might be obvious, but still worth mentioning: different audiences need different messages and different styles of design. Just like you use a different message when pitching your company to an investor versus a potential co-founder, you often need different words when talking to your customers and your providers—even if some people could be both.

In the beginning, you should focus on the most important customer segment: your early adopter users. As we mentioned in the previous chapter, launching an MVP means "selling the vision and delivering the minimum feature set to visionaries, not everyone". These visionaries are the *earlyvangelists* we mentioned earlier.

Drawing inspiration from the most successful marketplace businesses can be worthwhile. We are now going to take a look at two very popular marketplaces and how they communicate their value proposition to their target audience.

Case study 1: BlaBlaCar

Popular ridesharing service BlaBlaCar boasts more than 20 million users. In 2015, they raised $200 million in venture funding at a $1.6 billion valuation.

---

60   www.sharetribe.com/booklinks, #57

They facilitate rides for more than two million people every month. Let's take a look at their landing page at the time.

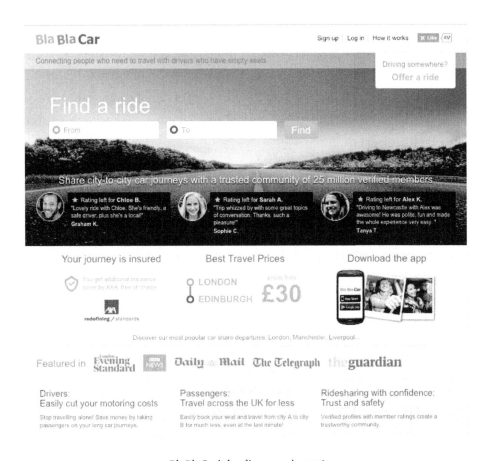

BlaBlaCar's landing page in 2016

You immediately notice the main value proposition, "Find a ride". There's also a call to action right next to the main form: a "Find" button to see the available rides for the desired route.

This is a really simple value proposition for customers—an easy way to get from place A to place B. It seems that BlaBlaCar has identified that their method of user acquisition is to first get people to book a ride in someone else's car, and after that convince them to offer rides themselves. You can see the secondary, smaller call to action ("Offer a ride") for providers in the top right corner of the page.

Under the main value proposition are three photos of BlaBlaCar users along with their testimonials, supporting the proposition. This is a typical "social proof" approach—people are more likely to believe their peers rather than the words of the company itself. The pictures also show that BlaBlaCar has identified their main target audience: younger people who want to save money while travelling and do not mind the social interaction with the driver and other passengers.

BlaBlaCar has separate landing pages for each country in which it operates. Each of these pages contains testimonials from local people, making it easier for new users to identify with them. Below the testimonials are additional value propositions. Finding a ride with BlaBlaCar is not only easy, but will also save you money. Travelling is safe because of the provided insurance.

BlaBlaCar makes these propositions explicit for both customers and providers: the providers (drivers) can "easily cut their motoring costs" while the customers (passengers) can "travel across their country for less".

BlaBlaCar also communicates additional value propositions in subtle ways. It uses a bright color scheme, with light green and blue as the main colors. This communicates its positive impact on the environment. The name of the brand itself and the playful logo communicate the positive social aspects of sharing a ride with strangers, something that works well with its youngish user segment. These design choices would not work for every marketplace. A marketplace that deals with money—like Lending Club—wants to appear as trustworthy as a bank, meaning calm blue and grey colors are justified.

While using BlaBlaCar, Cristóbal has talked to multiple passengers who said they first used the service due to the expected economic value or convenience. However, after using it, the additional value propositions started becoming more important. Drivers and passengers keep using the platform because they enjoy the resulting conversations, and can even form long-term friendships with other passengers.

This social value is a key retention factor for BlaBlaCar, but they don't emphasize it in their core messaging. While it makes people return to the service, the value proposition that originally gets the users hooked is related to convenience, trust, and price.

Case study 2: Wallapop

Wallapop (which merged with LetGo in 2016, raising $100M in the merger) is another great example of clarity when communicating a marketplace value proposition. Wallapop's marketplace app lets users buy and sell items nearby. The idea is not very original, but their execution is brilliant. When they launched, there were many other similar apps with comparable geolocation-based approaches. Why did they succeed?

One of the key factors was their excellent niche marketing strategy. Their first TV commercial, launched in April 2014, is a masterpiece of communicating the value proposition to a niche audience. At the time, they had thousands of users and enough resources to create any kind of commercial. They could have chosen to target the mainstream audience, but instead focused on only one segment: the young and cool "hipsters". Why?

Wallapop had identified that this segment was the most active in buying and selling second hand products in offline marketplaces. Wallapop knew these people would be the perfect earlyvangelist segment for them. Instead of going directly for the mass market, they chose to first become really successful in one niche, and then expand.

In the playful and cheeky video—which speaks the language and plays the music of its target audience—you notice three main value propositions:

- Geolocation: An easy way to find items nearby and ask around to get what you need.
- Economic value: The best deals to buy things their target audience love, like vintage glasses and bikes.
- Social value: Using Wallapop, you can meet your neighbours.

Beyond the landing page

In this chapter, we have focused on your landing page, but most of the key points apply to all your communications with your users—from support emails to error pages. They should all have the same coherent language and style.

Whether it's about the tone of voice, the color scheme, or the essential call to actions, always keep in mind who you're designing for, what your core value proposition to them is, and what are the key actions you want your users to take in each case. This helps you create a consistent experience throughout your platform.

How to do it yourself

Let's use the familiar example from the previous chapters: a marketplace for personal training services. For the providers, your core message is likely about getting more business.

Meanwhile, for customers, you probably want to focus on the ease of finding the right trainer.

Since most of your users are customers, you figure that the most important function of your main landing page is customer acquisition.

Providers are easier to acquire by hand. This means your main call to action should be directed towards your customers. In the case of personal trainers, you identified the most promising early segment is "wealthy stay-at-home moms between the age of 30 and 50". They don't care that much about saving money, but they do care about the quality of the service, and saving time.

You could start with a big slogan like "Find the right trainer for you today" near the top of the page. Or you could drill down even deeper into the needs of your target users. Why do they want to find personal trainers? Because they want to get in shape. You could say something like "The easiest way to get fit". After the slogan, it's a good idea to have a big call to action, just like in BlaBlaCar's case. The most logical approach is to ask your users to enter their location.

On the design side, in general, big images work really well. In this case, you could use a photo of a person who belongs to your target segment training at the gym, with the trainer giving her instructions. If you do not have a suitable photo available, many stock photo sites provide affordable quality photos, and provide you with the ability to filter their collection of photos based on things like sex, ethnicity and age to find one that matches your audience. We recommend using Stocksy.

As soon as you have your first users, you should add their stories, in their own language. Ideally, their experiences match the story you want to tell your prospective customers.

Below the propositions to your customers, you can talk about the benefits for trainers: "Get new customers by advertising your services on our site for free!" You could also have a secondary call to action for trainers to sign up at the top of your page.

Another option to consider is to have a separate, secondary landing page for trainers. This lets you focus on explaining your value proposition to them in a clear, more direct way, and also gives you an excellent place to point potential trainers to if you decide to target them with advertising.

Summary

In this chapter, we have discussed the impact of language and design on your ability to communicate your main value proposition and making a good first impression. This is a critical first step in making users stay on your platform.

We are now going to shift our focus towards the design of your marketplace. By "design", we do not mean simply making your marketplace look pretty; as famously said by Steve Jobs, "Design is not just what it looks like and feels like. Design is how it works." We will dig deeper into practices that actually make your marketplace work for your users.

As you've learned by now, the most important job of a marketplace is to facilitate transactions between its users. To make this happen, you need to be able to *match the customer with the right provider*, and *guide them through the transaction process*. Chapter 9 will focus on matchmaking and in chapter 10 we'll take a look at the transaction itself.

9

How to match your customers with the right providers

In the previous chapter, we discussed how to effectively communicate the value of your marketplace. Now that you've earned your users' attention, it's time to deliver on your promise.

Your first job is to help customers find the product or service they're looking for. Of course, whatever they're looking for needs to exist on the site, meaning you need to have enough supply. But even if the product or service is available, that does not guarantee that the customer will be able to find it. You need to make careful design decisions to make finding a specific product as effortless as possible.

Jonathan Goulden, former director of product at Airbnb, says[61] that of the most important questions that define every marketplace is understanding whether you have homogenous or heterogenous supply. In the former case, every provider is the same from the customer's point of view, which means that the marketplace can choose the right provider for the customer automatically. This greatly simplifies the customer experience, but also makes the marketplace concept easier to copy; the quality of the supply matters less. Goulden calls

---

61   www.sharetribe.com/booklinks, #58

these marketplaces "matching marketplaces". Delivery marketplaces like Uber and Instacart are examples of matching marketplaces.

Most marketplaces fall under the heterogenous supply category, or what Goulden calls "search marketplaces". All product marketplaces are like this: the user always needs to compare different products and their prices. Most service marketplaces also fall into this category. If you're looking for someone to write you a piece of software, renovate your home or babysit your children, there are so many criteria that apply only to you that automatic matching (usually) becomes impossible. As matching marketplaces are so rare, we'll focus mostly on search marketplaces in this article.

In search marketplaces, the first thing your prospective customers will typically do is one of two actions: either type in a search query, or click on a product category. They then start refining their search with filters or by sorting the results based on the attribute that is most relevant to them. The resulting display of results is usually shown as a list or on a map.

We will now go through the different elements of a good product discovery experience—search, categories, filters, sorting, and displaying—and discuss best practices related to each. As always, there is no single design that will work for all use cases—marketplaces are very different from each other. We will help you design an experience that best suits your specific marketplace idea.

Building your marketplace's search engine

When a customer lands on your site, search is likely their first action. It makes sense; typing in what you are looking for is the most intuitive and easiest action to take. If search engines were perfect, search alone would suffice: by describing your exact needs in your own words, the search engine would always understand what you are looking for.

Unfortunately, building a perfect search engine is impossible. It requires developing advanced artificial intelligence algorithms to not only understand what people say, but what they mean. Thus, in most cases, we are stuck with more basic solutions: we type in a keyword and get back a list of products that have the said keyword in their product description or other metadata.

In some cases, what is searched for might not be the product itself but the product or service's location. Airbnb is a good example—you start by entering your destination city to get a list of all available apartments in that location. Let us go over these two types of search.

Keyword search

Customers expect the keyword search bar to be located at the very top of your site. It makes sense to include it on just about every page of your site to let users search whenever the need arises. The exception to this is the checkout path. Once someone is ready to perform a transaction, the search bar might be a distraction.

Having a clear placeholder text with instructions inside the search bar is also a good idea. For example, you might have: "Search for products by keyword or product code."

The key to making search work well is relevancy: the order in which the results are shown. For example, the search should return products with the keyword in the title first, followed by the ones where the keyword is in the description. Your search should be able to return partial matches ("bike" should be able to find "motorbike"), but it should put more emphasis on exact matches. Because of spelling mistakes, having "fuzzy matching"—returning results that almost match the query—is a plus.

Another search feature that may be useful is autocompletion, which suggests keywords as the customer types in their search query. The point of the feature is not to make searching faster, but to offer customers ideas about what kinds of keywords to use. While this can be very helpful, be warned: a study by Baymard, an institute that conducts research on e-commerce usability, found that 36% of autocomplete implementations do more harm than good[62]. As a

---

62   www.sharetribe.com/booklinks, #59

rule of thumb, you should be very selective about what kind of suggestions to include and should not use previous search entries to generate suggestions.

Since search is one of the most commonly performed actions by your customers, you should track how they use it. Keep a list of the 10 most common keywords that are used and test them out yourself on your site. Are you happy with the results? If not, chances are your customers are not either. If this happens, you need to either increase supply with products that better match these searches, make sure you are attracting the right type of customers with your value proposition (see chapter 8), help your suppliers use better keywords in their listings, or change the way your search works.

Location search

Location search finds products based on their physical location. When using location search, your customers should be able to search on different levels: from city or country names to zip codes and street addresses.

Location search should not only return exact matches, but results near the given location as well. If you search for a specific street name, you are likely interested in listings from nearby streets as well. The location search can be accompanied by a radius: do you want to find products within a range of 5 or 50 kilometers?

Generally, location search results are displayed on a map. If a list is used instead of a map, the results should be ordered based on their proximity to the location provided by the customer. In this scenario, the location search acts more like a sorting method.

Autocomplete is used more frequently with location search than keyword search, and with good reason: there are only a finite number of possible locations, making it easier to return relevant results. Location search engines like Google Maps can offer this feature out of the box.

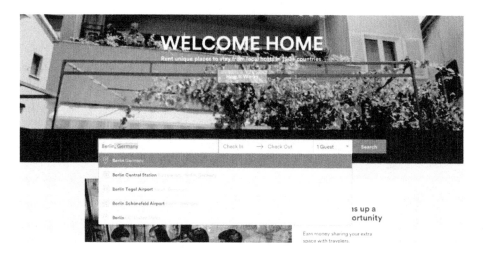

Airbnb makes location search easier with autocomplete

Some websites combine location and keyword search. This is typical in local classifieds sites like Gumtree. In these cases, one search is performed first, after which the results are filtered using the other search.

Defining your taxonomy with categories

When your customers know what they are looking for, search is the tool of choice. However, when this is not the case, being able to browse your selection becomes important. The typical first action is to select a relevant product category. Classified ads websites like Craigslist rely heavily on categories. When you open Craigslist, you are prompted with a long list of categories, clearly communicating that the logical first step is to select one of them.

Craigslist uses categories heavily

Categories are commonly used to define the structure of your site. They also guide your providers by telling them what kinds of products or services they should list. If they cannot find a suitable category for their wares, your site might not be the right place for their business.

Should search or categories be more prominent on your site? It depends. Typically, search is the top choice, but if your site does not have a huge selection, putting more emphasis on categories might make sense. It helps customers discover what is on offer and reduces the chance of customers being served an unfortunate "No search results" message.

Almost all traditional e-commerce sites have a hierarchical category structure, with categories, subcategories, sub-subcategories, and so on. A product usually belongs to only one category, though it can make sense to have a subcategory in multiple top-level categories.

Some more recent marketplaces are, however, doing away with the category structure entirely. This is particularly common among marketplaces that only feature very specific types of products or services.

Airbnb is a good example: instead of a hierarchical category structure, they use *faceted search*—a location search that can be narrowed down by using filters for different apartment features. We are going to talk more about filters later on.

If you decide to use categories, we recommend using them cautiously during the early days of your marketplace. Too often, we see budding marketplace founders take their cues from large e-commerce sites and create complex category structures with tens of top-level categories and dozens of subcategories. This is a good idea only if you expect to launch your site with thousands of products. Otherwise, it will only lead to frustration for your users. Browsing a complex category structure can be quite tedious, especially if most of them are empty.

A good rule of thumb is that no category should be empty when you launch your site to the first customers. If you do not have enough supply for 100 subcategories, consider only having 5-6 top-level categories and no subcategories. Without a vast array of products, this will be enough for your customers.

When you start acquiring more products and providers, you can add new categories and subcategories based on supply and demand. This supply-driven approach results in far better usability for your users.

Filtering the results

In order to find exactly what they are looking for, conducting a simple search or picking a category might not be enough for your customers. With lots of results, the customer needs to be able to filter results through various dimensions. This is called faceted search, and getting it right can be a complex task. In their studies, Baymard found that only 40% of e-commerce sites use faceted search at all, and only 16% of major e-commerce websites offer a reasonably good filtering experience[63].

---

63   www.sharetribe.com/booklinks, #59

A common error is the lack of category-specific filters. If your marketplace is about selling pre-owned shoes and purses, you might have a filter for shoe size. This makes sense for people looking for shoes, but not for those looking for bags. You should only display the shoe size filter for customers that are looking for shoes. This is common sense, but Baymard found that 42% of all e-commerce websites do not take advantage of this strategy.

The great part about filters is that they can be used to classify your products in various ways. For instance, you could use so-called *thematic filters*. If we continue with the shoes example, one theme could be whether the shoes are suitable for winter or summer. This classification is not well suited for a traditional category structure, but for some customers, it may be the critical factor in their search. Another example is customers who are only interested Nike shoes and want to filter based on brand.

Just like with categories, be cautious when adding new filters. Every time you are considering adding a new filter, ask yourself: "Does this really improve the usability of my site?" If you add too many filters, your site's user interface easily becomes crowded and your customers will have a hard time finding the filter they are looking for.

Additionally, when a marketplace does not have a large supply, customers are more likely to end up in a situation where a combination of filters returns no results. This, of course, should be avoided. Instead, start with only a few important filters, and add more later on (if needed). Testing your site with different search, category and filter combinations to see what kind of results they return is never a bad idea.

Sorting the results

Each of your customers is different. Some of them want the best product, no matter the cost. Others are more sensitive to price, and start searching from the cheaper end. A third group only wants to buy from reliable vendors—providers that have the best reviews. Yet another group visits your marketplace regularly and wants to browse the latest additions. One sorting method cannot cater to all these groups.

In general, the best default for search results is to sort by relevance: the results that are most relevant based on the query provided by the customer. If the user is browsing a category, you can show the newest products first, or even manually curate the listings to show the category's most important results first. If you do not have many products in your marketplace, this might suffice.

However, as the number of products grows, options to sort by publishing date, price and provider's ratings may become useful. Validate this by talking to your customers; you do not want to increase the complexity of your site with a feature that no-one will use.

It is important to consider whether it is in your best interest to allow customers to sort based on a certain attribute. For instance, being able to sort by price might incentivize providers to reduce their prices to get to the top of the list. This, in turn, might lead to lower quality offerings. A viable alternative is to have a price filter for price-sensitive users.

Displaying the results

The two typical ways to display marketplace offerings are a list and a map. Maps are oftentimes shown side by side with a list.

As a list

The most common way to show products in a list is using a grid of big product images. This makes a lot of sense: quality photos play a huge role in making your marketplace visually appealing. Emphasis should be placed on this aspect in the early days of your marketplace.

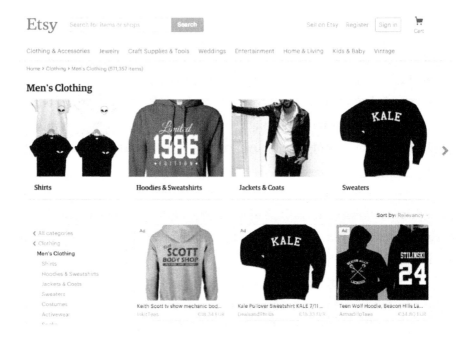

Etsy uses the classic grid model to display products

In a traditional grid, the product "cards" are all the same size. A twist on the traditional grid is to have varying heights for cards, as popularized by the social media site Pinterest. This format displays the entire image, which is especially useful on sites with lots of user-generated content. Some of your providers will use portrait images while others use landscape, which can lead to annoying cropping effects if all the cards need to be the same size.

However, the Pinterest-style grid has its downsides, especially in a marketplace context. It is an effective presentation format when users need to quickly browse through visual content, but is not as well suited when they need to find a specific product. The variety of heights can feel chaotic and hinder usability. Performance issues may also arise when positioning the product images correctly. For these reasons, we do not recommend this approach for most marketplaces. Etsy tried using it in the past but eventually gave up, potentially due to these reasons.

If the products or services in your marketplace cannot be photographed easily, a simple list might be a better alternative to a grid. Oppex, for instance, is a marketplace for public tenders that do not have suitable product photos.

However, if in any way possible possible, coming up with a creative way to use photos for listings helps make your site more visually appealing. For example, if your providers offer intangible services like business consulting or coaching, they could simply use their profile photo as the product photo.

For product cards, a good design tip is to show as little information as necessary. This makes it easier for the customer to quickly find the most important information and keeps your marketplace clutter-free.

The most essential attributes are listing title and price (if there is one). An image should definitely be displayed if one is available. To emphasize that your marketplace aggregates products from individual users instead of traditional e-commerce businesses, including their profile photo and name can be a good idea. If your providers are companies, you could display their logos instead. If trust is especially important in your marketplace, you could display the rating of each provider next to their name. If your marketplace is location-based, distance information can be useful for users. These basic options should cover most common cases. Do not add a long product description to the cards—they will only make your site look crowded and create unnecessary noise.

There are three main approaches to handling browsing. The most traditional one is pagination: you display a set number of results with links to move to other result pages. Baymard found that customers perceive pagination to be a slow way to browse, and quite often leads to them never going beyond the first page. In some cases, that may be your target. If you feel that the first 20 results of your search are the most relevant ones and are the ones your customer should focus on, hiding the rest of the results behind pagination can be a good strategy.

However, in most cases, it makes sense to let your customers browse all the results easily. Pagination is especially problematic if users want to compare multiple products quickly, as it might involve going back and forth between different pages.

Infinite scroll is a popular way to speed up browsing. It works by automatically loading new results as the user scrolls down the page. Another option is to offer a load more button at the end of the results list, allowing the customer to decide whether they want to see more results. If the user clicks the button, the results are added directly below the last results instead of loading a new page.

Baymard has found that the best option is to combine infinite scroll and a load more button: first show 10 to 30 products, then keep adding another 10-30 products as the user scrolls down—the exact amount depends on the context of your marketplace—until you reach 50-100 products. Once at the bottom, you should display a load more button.

Why this combination? One problem with infinite scrolling is that it prevents the use of a footer on your website. As the user scrolls towards the bottom of the page, new products are automatically loaded and push the footer further away. To use a footer on your site, you need to give your users a break from infinite scrolling every now and then. To continue loading more products, they can click on the load more button.

Furthermore, when displaying search results, it is a good idea to focus on the items that have the highest relevance. Using the load more button allows you to do this since it gives less emphasis to the results that come after the button.

On a map

When displaying a map, the important thing to decide is how big an area should be shown on the map—in other words, how "zoomed in" your map should be. If you use the Google Maps API for location-based searches, it helps by returning a "bounding box" based on the analysis it performs on the search query. Google understands whether the customer wants a smaller or a bigger area, and shows a map at the relevant zoom level based on this.

Many modern marketplaces offer a way to refresh the location search when the user moves the map. This is a convenient way to refine a location search without having to enter the search query multiple times. It is definitely a recommended practice if you plan on using location search. The list and map should work together: if the map is moved, the list should be refreshed as well.

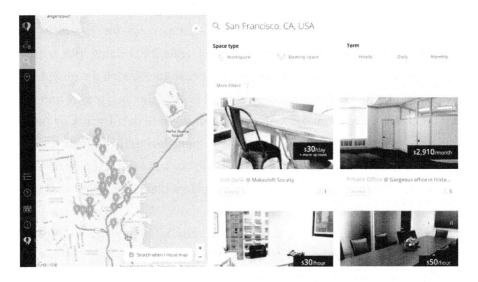

Sharedesk uses a map and list that work together

The list and map can act together in other ways as well. An example: when you hover over a pin on the map, the list could scroll down to that particular listing. Conversely, if you hover over a listing, the map could highlight that listing. This conveys helpful information to the customer, as they're able to quickly compare both location and listing information.

In a combined list and map view, the most common way to browse is with pagination. The reason is practical: the list and map should always display the same listings, and the map may become crowded if the user scrolls down a long way with infinite scroll. However, infinite scrolling and a load more button can sometimes be used, too.

Reverse marketplaces

Some service marketplaces require complex negotiations between a customer and a provider before the parties can agree on pricing, schedule, and other details. Typical examples include knowledge work like software development and design or home services like plumbing or electricians. In these cases, having to contact and go through a negotiation process with a large number of providers is not exactly the best experience for customers.

In such situations, the marketplace can consider turning the search experience on its head: instead of having the customer search for providers, they make providers search for customers. The way this is typically done is that the customer is first asked to describe their needs in detail by asking them a series of questions. After this, a job offer is published to the providers, who can then make bids on it. We call this a "reverse marketplace". Thumbtack and Upwork are examples of well-known marketplaces that employ this kind of a reverse search workflow.

The same principles described in this article also apply to reverse marketplaces. The key difference is that you need to design the search experience from the perspective of the provider and their needs.

Putting it all together with an example

It is now time to apply everything that we have learned in this chapter to our example marketplace from previous chapters: a marketplace for personal training services.

The automatic "on-demand" approach does not really work in this case. The level of service between different providers may vary dramatically, with each having their own style. Customers will want to be able to compare different providers. At the same time, the offerings of the providers can be packaged well enough, so a traditional search workflow can be used instead of a reverse one.

The first decision is whether to use a keyword or a location search. With personal training services, location is important: you want to find a trainer near your home or workplace. Meanwhile, it is not exactly clear what would be searched for with a keyword search. Thus, a location search is the logical option.

Using categories makes sense. They are an effective way to describe the main attribute of the service being offered. You could start with a single-level hierarchy, and add a second level later on if needed. For example, the top level could be combat sports, with karate, judo and so on below it.

You should also add a few key filters that describe the most important dimensions. Price is an obvious one. Your customers have different budgets, so they should be able to filter based on the maximum price they are able to pay. Another logical dimension is the level of training: are you a beginner or a professional athlete? Filtering based on gender might also be relevant for some customers. With these three filters, you should be good to go. Sort options are not required as the location search handles that part well enough.

The most logical way to display the results is with a side by side map and list. The list should be a grid, with plenty of emphasis on photos. The trainers can provide photos of their training sessions or simply use photos of themselves. The best browsing style option is pagination as you do not want to display too many results on the map at once.

Summary

In this chapter, we learned about how to match your customers with the right providers. In some cases, any provider can do the job, which means the marketplace can handle matching automatically. In most cases, you need to provide your customers with a way to search for the right provider.

We then went over the elements of a typical provider discovery process: search, categories, filters, sorting, and displaying the results.

Search is the most important call to action for your customers. The first decision you need to make is between a keyword and location search. Categories can be useful in structuring your site, but it can make sense to skip them entirely, using filters with various dimensions instead.

Sorting by relevance is generally a good enough default sorting option, but if your marketplace has lots of products, other criteria for sorting can be useful. The two most typical ways to display the products or services are a list and a map.

As with many other things, "less is more" applies to discovery as well. Especially in the early days of your marketplace (when your supply is limited), not having too many categories or filters is a good idea—they can be distractions, and can lead to disappointment if no products are found.

Start with the basics, and add a more comprehensive structure as your marketplace grows and your customers start giving you feedback about their needs.

10

How to design your marketplace's transaction flow

In the previous chapter, you learned how to match your customer and provider. Now that the match has been made, how can you facilitate the transaction?

Many early-stage marketplace entrepreneurs pay a lot of attention to how many users sign up for their marketplace. This is a mistake.

User count is a so-called vanity metric—one that doesn't tell you if the marketplace is actually satisfying your users' needs. As mentioned before, the purpose of any marketplace is to facilitate transactions between users. Without transactions, your marketplace doesn't provide value to anyone.

We define a transaction as an exchange of value between a customer and provider. The transaction may involve money, it may be a barter, or the provider can offer their product or service for free.

The number one goal for any marketplace is high "liquidity". This quote by Simon Rothman bears repeating: "Liquidity isn't the most important thing. It's the only thing."[64] Rothman defines liquidity as "the reasonable expectation of selling something you list or finding what you are looking for".

---

64   www.sharetribe.com/booklinks, #60

High liquidity—in other words, lots of transactions and lots of provided value—should result in happy users. To reach high liquidity on your platform, transactions need to be seamless. It's not enough to match the customer and the provider. Many things can still go wrong after they've found each other. You need to help them transact easily and securely.

In this chapter, we will talk about ways of ensuring the transaction actually ends up happening.

Making the payment

The first thing to decide is whether completing the transaction involves an online payment through your marketplace or not. As we discussed in chapter three, capturing the payment is often essential for your business model, so the answer is usually yes.

Unfortunately, online payment is also a major source of friction during the transaction, which is why some popular marketplaces like Thumbtack and OfferUp have decided to skip it altogether. They reason that they want to facilitate a maximum number of transactions, and do not want online payment getting in the way. On those sites, the customer and provider simply form an agreement and complete the actual exchange of money outside the platform.

If you decide that a payment through your platform is necessary, you will need to select a payment method, define the steps of the checkout process, and choose the point at which the payment occurs.

How to choose the right payment method

Credit cards are the most common method of payment since they are used globally. They are especially suitable for online payments because credit card companies usually provide coverage for customers in case of fraud.

In some countries, paying with a direct bank transfer (or wire transfer) is more popular than paying with a credit card. However, bank transfers are usually not as convenient for marketplaces as they lack features such as fraud protection or the ability to preauthorize payments (more on this later).

PayPal is another well-known global payment method. In some countries, PayPal is available for people who do not have a credit card. PayPal often has higher fees than credit card processing companies, but it also offers additional services, like a protection program for both customers and providers.

Handling online payments is a heavily regulated area. Building your payment system may involve a lot of bureaucracy. If you want your providers to be able to accept credit card payments, you need to either become PCI compliant (which is a very heavy process) or use a payment gateway that handles the bureaucracy for you.

When choosing a gateway, you should pay special attention to whether the gateway handles the special features required by marketplaces, like splitting payments between you and your providers, and handling the regulatory requirements like know your customer (KYC) and anti-money laundering processes automatically for all your providers. This can be a tricky issue for marketplaces where the providers are individuals since the providers might not be willing to go through a heavy compliance process. You should choose a payment provider that provides a smooth onboarding experience for everyone.

Today, many payment gateway companies have solutions designed specifically for building marketplaces. Stripe, Braintree, MangoPay, Adyen and PayPal all offer such solutions. Each has its own pros and cons. There are at least four main factors you should consider when choosing your provider:

- Supported currencies and countries. You want to make sure that your gateway is able to move money to providers in each country where you operate, in the local currency.
- Fees. Each provider has a different fee structure. The fees can depend on several things, like the monthly volume of the marketplace, the monthly volume of each provider, or the size of an average transaction. You might want to do some calculations based on these figures to find the best choice for you.
- Features. As an example, does the gateway provide the ability to delay the payout to the provider (more on this later)? You might also

want to ask them about dealing with chargebacks, fraud protection, or handling deposits.

- Ease of development. It can take a lot of development work to build an integration to a payment gateway, so the quality of their developer tools matter a lot. If you're using an existing marketplace software with a built-in integration, you don't need to worry about this.

The steps of the checkout process

The checkout process is the set of actions required from the customer to select a product or service, complete the exchange and (if online payments are used) make the payment. In traditional e-commerce, the most popular checkout experience involves a shopping cart. The customer adds all the desired products to the cart and proceeds to checkout when they are done shopping. If you expect the bulk of your users to make multiple purchases in one session, this approach is a great choice.

Many modern marketplaces have noticed that a shopping cart is unnecessary for them. If the marketplace offers rentals, services, or pre-owned products, a shopping cart is far less common. After all, it introduces an extra step: you need to add the product to the cart before being able to proceed to checkout.

A good rule of thumb is that you should have as few checkout steps as possible. When using Airbnb, there is no "add to cart" action—when you see something you want, you move to the booking page instantly.

A study by Baymard, the e-commerce usability research institute, found that at least 59.8% of potential customers abandon their shopping cart[65]. This clearly shows that it is not enough to get people to start the checkout process. People will often not follow through, especially if the process is complicated. Baymard's large study[66] has lots of detailed information on how to improve the

---

65   www.sharetribe.com/booklinks, #61
66   www.sharetribe.com/booklinks, #62

usability of the process. Again, looking at Airbnb[67], the simplest checkout can be a one-page experience.

An interesting question is whether registration should be mandatory during checkout or not. One would think that skipping the registration or login step is a good idea to make checkout easier. However, most popular marketplaces like Etsy and Airbnb require you to sign up before you can proceed to checkout. They seem to have arrived at the conclusion that the benefit of acquiring a new user outweighs the cost of a potentially lost transaction. Getting more information about users might also be important in preventing fraud.

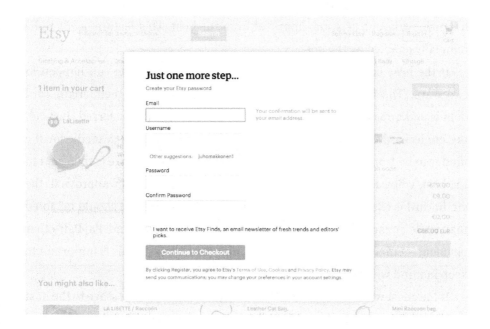

Etsy requires users to sign up before continuing with the checkout

When should the money be transferred?

On traditional e-commerce sites, the money is transferred immediately after checkout is completed. This process is ideal if the availability and exact

---

67   www.sharetribe.com/booklinks, #63

price of the product are known beforehand. This is usually the case when you are buying a physical product that is shipped to you.

However, transferring the money immediately does not work as well with rental or service marketplaces. Consider Airbnb. The hosts generally want to review and approve whoever is booking their place before any money exchanges hands. The host may have forgotten to keep their booking calendar up to date, and the place might not be available after all. In some cases, the guest may want to negotiate the final price before paying.

Airbnb offers three different checkout flows. The first one is instant booking, which works just like a traditional e-commerce site: the payment happens without a separate approval from the host. This feature needs to be manually enabled by the host.

If the host has not enabled instant booking, the booking can happen in two ways. The first is preauthorization: the guest enters their credit card details and approves the payment, but the money is not transferred. Instead, the credit card company guarantees that the card has enough credit for the money to be transferred during the next seven days. A message is then sent to the host, who can either approve or reject the booking. If they approve it, the credit card is charged. If they reject it, no transfer is made. It should be noted that while preauthorization is possible with credit cards and PayPal, other payment methods (like bank transfers) might not allow it. This is important to keep in mind when choosing your payment method.

If the guest wants to negotiate the price, they can send a message to the host with a proposal. The host can then pre-approve the price. The guest is notified and is prompted to make the payment, after which the money is transferred instantly. Instead of accepting the guest's offer, the host can also reject it or make a pre-approved counter-offer.

These Airbnb-style transaction flows can also be used in marketplaces that sell physical products. For instance, if the marketplace is used for selling pre-owned wedding dresses that can be tried on before buying, the providers might want to vet customers before letting them into their home. If a marketplace is used to sell custom-made products, a negotiation between the buyer and seller is often needed before deciding on a final price.

In some service marketplaces, transferring the money is even trickier. As an example, think of a marketplace for IT freelancers in which work is done by the hour. The customer only knows the hourly price beforehand, and the final price is tallied only after the project is done. Thumbtack often deals with these types of projects, which is likely a major reason why they have not handled online payments so far.

Sometimes it's not possible to know the exact price before the work is done. For instance, a programmer who charges by hour might not know how many hours exactly a task will take before it's finished. In such cases, it is possible to design a platform that allows the provider to invoice the customer after the work is done. However, as we have discussed in chapter four, this gives the provider the opportunity to easily bypass the marketplace's payment system by manually sending an invoice. Upwork has addressed the issue by giving providers enough helpful tools to make it worth their while to use the site's billing system.

Moving the money to the provider

In an online store, the transaction flow ends once the money is transferred from the customer. Marketplaces, on the other hand, are more complicated. The money needs to also be transferred to the provider. Despite tremendous advances over the past five years, as of this writing, this process is still surprisingly complicated. There are two main decisions you need to make here: when to move the money to the provider, and how to do it.

When to move the money to the provider

Your easiest option is to transfer the money directly to the provider once payment is made. There are, however, situations where this might not be the best solution. As we discussed in chapter eight, part of your value proposition might be to act as a trusted middleman who guarantees that the customer gets what they ordered. One way to go about this is to delay the provider payout until the customer confirms receipt of what was ordered.

There are many ways you can handle the relationship between your providers and customers. One is to become a service provider yourself, meaning the transaction essentially happens between you and the customer. This is what Uber does. The drivers are not in a direct financial relationship with the passengers. Uber guarantees the level of service and charges the money. The drivers have a financial relationship with Uber as contractors.

This is a viable approach, but it also means that Uber, as a platform, is responsible for everything that happens in their marketplace, including the level of service. It also opens up another can of worms: it is not obvious whether the providers are really independent contractors or employees. For instance, a UK court ruled in 2016[68] that Uber drivers are employees, not contractors. Classifying your providers as employees can be a huge financial and regulatory burden. To avoid all of this, it might be better to have the financial relationship be between the customer and the provider.

It is possible to delay the payout without being the service provider yourself. One way is through escrow, where you act as a trusted third party that holds the money for the parties involved. The challenge with this approach is the ensuing legal burden—escrow is a heavily regulated field. In the United States, escrow is regulated on the state level, meaning you might need to acquire a state license to be allowed to hold funds. This can be costly and time-consuming. Other countries have their own regulations.

Some payment gateways (like MangoPay) offer escrow solutions out of the box, which means you don't need to worry about licensing. However, this means their country support is often limited. As of this writing, MangoPay only offers escrow in providers in Europe, not in the US. Other providers (like Stripe) offer escrow-like solutions that allow you to delay the payout one way or another. This is an area where new solutions are entering the market

---

68   www.sharetribe.com/booklinks, #64

constantly; if the ability to delay the payout is important for you, be sure to check your payment gateway's latest position on the matter

How to move the money to the provider

Moving money to your providers sounds like an easy task. Unfortunately, it is not; this is yet another area that is heavily regulated to prevent money laundering.

Before you can move money to an individual, they first need to go through a process called know your customer (KYC) to verify their identity. The type of information needed depends on the country of the provider and how much money they will be receiving.

In general, it is possible to receive up to a few thousand dollars with a lighter review. If the provider expects to receive more money, a more thorough process is needed. Stripe has created a handy guide[69] about the minimum information that is needed for several countries. For a complete perspective on global payouts, you can refer to a comprehensive guide[70] put together by payout company Adyen.

The KYC process is likely one reason why marketplaces like OfferUp and Wallapop have decided to not offer an online payment system. They want to make it as frictionless as possible for individuals to sell used low-value items, and adding their financial information might be a key barrier that prevents providers from getting started.

From a regulatory perspective, managing multiple countries and currencies in one marketplace can be very tricky. This is one of the reasons why it's a good idea to start your marketplace in one country—or at least only have all your providers in the same country in the beginning—to avoid having to deal with regulatory differences between countries.

If you want to charge a commission for the transaction, you need to decide when and how to charge it. As we discussed above, from a regulatory

---

69   www.sharetribe.com/booklinks, #65
70   www.sharetribe.com/booklinks, #66

perspective, receiving all the money and transferring the provider's part to them can be difficult. If you want to avoid this hassle, you should either split the payment into two separate transactions—one goes to the provider and another to you—or move the whole amount to the provider and charge your commission fee from them after the transaction.

An example transaction flow

It is now time to put what you have learned into practice and design the checkout transaction flow for the imaginary marketplace from our previous chapters: a marketplace for personal trainers.

The first decision is whether you want to offer an online payment option or not. Since we had decided (in chapter six) that online payment is one of the main value propositions for your trainers, handling payments on your platform is definitely important.

You expect your customers to make repeat purchases through your site and believe reviews are important for the success of your platform. Because of this, you decide to ask customers to log in before they can make a booking. As booking multiple providers at the same time is not a common use case, a shopping cart is not needed. Instead, your customers can book and make a payment directly from the trainer's profile page. You opt for a simple, one-page checkout process that lets customers review all the details at a glance.

Since trainers manage their availability on your site using a calendar, you can allow the customer to make the booking and preauthorize the payment directly without negotiating with the provider. You decide that the providers should be able to choose their customers, so you add a step to let the trainers accept the booking before the money is moved.

You decide to improve your value proposition by acting as a trusted middleman who holds the money until the training session has taken place successfully. You choose Stripe Connect to power your payment system since it has relatively low fees, a simple onboarding for your providers, an easy way to delay payouts, and the ability to easily split payments so you can charge your commission.

Summary

This chapter focused on how to make transactions as easy as possible for the users of your platform. There are several steps in any marketplace's transaction process, and decisions need to be made about each one.

The checkout flow should be as short and simple as possible. The first decision is whether to use online payments or not. The most typical payment methods are by credit card, bank transfers, wire transfer, and PayPal. You should only move the money from the customer when you are sure the transaction will happen.

Moving money to your providers can be surprisingly challenging, mostly due to regulation. If you want to hold money for others, you might need an escrow license. Alternatively, you can become the service provider and make your providers your contractors (or employees), or charge the credit card only after the service has been provided. Your providers will need to go through a verification process before you can move money to them, which can be an issue for marketplaces where individuals trade low-value items.

We've now gotten through the basics of designing your marketplace platform. Now it's time to get people to use it! In the remaining six chapters, we will focus on strategies for launching your platform, building your user base, and growing your business.

11

How to build the initial supply

In the previous chapter, you learned how to build the transaction flow of your marketplace. Now it's time to start onboarding the first providers to your platform.

Compared to traditional e-commerce, most of a marketplace's unique challenges come from the marketplace having two sides to it: customers and providers. When launching a two-sided marketplace, this means you need to solve the "chicken and egg problem"—how to get customers with little supply and how to get supply with only a few customers. In our opinion, this is the biggest challenge any marketplace faces.

In almost all cases, it makes sense to start building a marketplace's audience from the supply side. Because of this, the best way to solve a marketplace's chicken and egg problem is to "seed" the marketplace. You should focus on signing up your providers and getting them to list their products or services, building up a relative large base of initial supply before inviting a single customer. In fact, trying to grow both sides of the marketplace early on is a common mistake for marketplace entrepreneurs[71].

Why supply first? There are several reasons. As Boris Wertz and Angela Tran Kingyens explain in their comprehensive Guide to Marketplaces[72], providers

---

71   www.sharetribe.com/booklinks, #67
72   www.sharetribe.com/booklinks, #68

typically have a bigger incentive to join a marketplace than customers due to it being a major source of revenue for them. In The Online Economy[73], Philip Hu notes that providers transact more frequently. One provider can almost always serve a relative large number of customers, meaning you can make do with a smaller group of suppliers than customers.

Hu also notes that idle providers are less dangerous than idle customers. He writes:

> – *Airbnb hosts who have trouble renting out their rooms might choose to post on Craigslist or Homeaway simultaneously, but they are unlikely to leave the platform altogether, given the low cost of keeping a posting open. The perception that they might get business once in a while can be enough to motivate them to stay with Airbnb. On the other hand, for a traveler looking for lodging on any given night, she will perform the purchase off-platform if she can't find a suitable seller on Airbnb. Not only do buyers tend to have more alternatives than sellers because institutional sellers exist (hotels, taxis, etc.), but also buyers are harder to retain because of their less frequent transactions.*

In this chapter, we are going to go over common strategies for seeding marketplaces that do not yet have customers. First, we are going to discuss how to identify and find your first providers. We will then help you approach them in the correct fashion and convince them to list on your site. We are also going to discuss strategies for "faking" initial supply if getting providers onboard proves to be difficult.

How to find your first providers

Your first job is to figure out the best way to find suitable early-stage providers. Wertz and Kingyens identify numerous strategies, which we will now take a look at.

---

73   http://www.onlineeconomy.org/

Contact providers who are active in other marketplaces

Your providers are likely already active in forums or other marketplaces. Want to build a marketplace for pre-owned baby clothes? Check out all the Facebook groups dedicated to this purpose. They will be filled with potential providers.

Airbnb used this strategy in their early days. They would email people who were listing their apartment on Craigslist, asking them to also consider listing on Airbnb. GrowthHackers.com has put together an excellent case study[74] on Airbnb's growth strategy for details about their early growth efforts.

It is important for your marketplace to have a solid value proposition (see chapter eight) for the providers you contact. You need to be able to offer them something that is way better than the existing alternative. In Airbnb's case, when compared to Craigslist, they offered a better user experience and a much more trustworthy environment in which to conduct the transaction. We will review some of the common early stage value proposition strategies for providers later in this chapter.

Use Google, business directories, or offline aggregators

You might be in a situation where you are creating a completely unique marketplace—at least in your area—and don't have a ready source of providers from existing marketplace sites. If this is the case, the strategy to find providers depends on the types of providers you are planning to target.

Finding professional service providers (like plumbers or hairdressers) should not be too difficult as most of them will likely have some kind of online presence. Even if they do not have their own website, they should be listed in a business directory. You could start from sites like Yelp or the Yellow Pages in the US, or simply use Google. You should be able to compile a big enough list with these methods.

---

74   www.sharetribe.com/booklinks, #70

Depending on the profession, you might be able to find "offline aggregators". If you want to reach hairdressers, you can walk into the biggest hair salons. If you want to reach freelancers who build websites, you could try going to the local coworking space or finding a suitable Meetup group.

Etsy used the strategy of approaching offline aggregators successfully in their early days. As Danielle Maveal, Etsy's former director of seller education, writes on Quora:

> – *We got off the internet and there was a team out there across the U.S. and Canada attending art/craft shows nearly every weekend. Supporting potential sellers (we would buy them lunch, drop off 'craft show kits', pass out handmade promos)—these were artists/crafters that were influential in the handmade world. We knew if they set up shop on Etsy, and were successful, others would follow.*[75]

Sometimes the data might be available but scattered all over the web, so you need to put in a bit more effort to find it. Thumbtack wanted to reach a large number of service providers in different categories, and no suitable existing directory was available, so they built their own web crawler for aggregating the data.

Find people through online forums, networks, or Facebook groups

Let's say you are building a peer-to-peer marketplace that rents aerial drones. Your potential providers are drone owners who (most likely) have never considered renting their drones. These people cannot be found by using Google, business directories or other marketplaces.

However, these people are likely to hang out in certain online destinations, like popular drone-related blogs, bulletin boards, or Facebook groups. Perhaps they use a specific Instagram hashtag or follow a prolific video blogger on YouTube.

---

75   www.sharetribe.com/booklinks, #71

Conduct some research on your target audience. Find the places where they gather with other like-minded people. You should be able to find a media channel or a local group that caters to your specific audience to help you reach a big group of providers at once.

Be creative in thinking about what is the right community or network to tap into. Dan Martell, founder of Clarity, says that for them, SlideShare was how they found most of their early providers[76].

How to convince the providers to list on your marketplace

Now that you have found people to contact, how can you convince them to list their products or services on your platform? After all, you still do not have any customers on your platform, and listing requires some effort from the providers.

At this point, it is important to do things that don't scale. If possible, meet your first 50 to 100 providers in person. Take an hour with them to show how your platform works and explain your unique value proposition to them. Help them build their profile, list their products or services, and listen to their feedback. This approach is slow, but it is a great way to get to know your providers, receive feedback on your product (remember, you're still in the process of validating your concept), and ensure the quality of the initial supply.

Your core value proposition is likely tied to the number of customers on your platform. Before you can deliver on that promise, there are other incentives you can (and should) mention to get the providers to join.

Better than existing solutions

If your providers are active in other marketplaces, they already understand the basic value proposition of a marketplace. Your job is to communicate to them why your offering is better than the alternatives. As a refresher, below

---

76   www.sharetribe.com/booklinks, #72

are some of the ways in which you can provide a better value proposition. You need to focus on these aspects in your communication towards providers.

One option is to focus on trust. Airbnb improved on Craigslist by increasing the trust between hosts and guests. Today, they offer insurance and payment processing to prevent fraud. They also provided a smoother user experience for hosts, making the site more appealing than Craigslist's "classic" look and feel.

Lower fees for providers is another way to outdo the competition. This is how Etsy managed to get people from eBay: the seller would keep a bigger portion of the total price. Most of today's big marketplaces have a growing pressure to increase profits, and your opportunity lies in their margins. You can emphasize this benefit by offering early-bird discounts. For instance, give a six month 50% fee discount for the first 100 providers who sign up.

As we discussed in chapter 4, you could also consider offering your providers a stake in your company. This is how Stocksy was able to undercut incumbent stock photo marketplaces. Professional photographer Thomas Hawk explains his rationale for leaving Getty Images for Stocksy as follows:

> – *The exciting part about Stocksy though isn't just the higher payout, it's that the members of Stocksy actually OWN the agency. That's right, after paying out costs, Stocksy will distribute profits to its members— so members will get dividends and actually hold real equity in the business*[77].

Offer exclusivity

In the early days of your marketplace, you will only have a few providers. While this has obvious downsides, you can also use this to your advantage. You could make your marketplace an exclusive club, stating that only the best providers will be accepted. You can vet each provider manually before letting them in. When you invite new people, you can tell them they have been selected

---

77   www.sharetribe.com/booklinks, #73

based on very specific criteria, and only the very best will get this invite. For reference, we encourage you to benchmark the provider application processes of successful marketplace companies[78].

There are multiple benefits to this approach. First, it creates buzz in the provider community. People will talk to each other about such opportunities, and having restricted access instantly makes your offering more interesting. Everyone wants to be part of an exclusive club. To your providers, exclusivity means better publicity, which means they will soon be competing for your attention.

Moreover, focusing on quality instead of quantity is an important business move. It is better to have ten quality providers than 100 lousy ones. Since they will be your *earlyvangelists*, you want to make sure that all your early customers will have a great experience. It is better to scale only when you know you can keep the customer experience at a high enough level. As a bonus, the best providers will bring new customers with them[79].

EatWith, a marketplace for home-cooked dinners, has been focusing on quality instead of quantity since they started, and it has been an effective strategy for them. They are currently a category leader in their crowded space. Even today, they only accept 3% of cooks who apply to join. Stocksy is another platform that has used this approach effectively. As Thomas Hawk mentions in his blog post, quality was another important reason for him to join Stocksy:

> – *Even if you don't care [about owning shares], still give Stocksy a look, because the imagery there really is miles ahead of what you see in the run of the mill stock photography library out there today.*

Finally, having a vetting process in place means you will have a good excuse to talk to each provider. This means that you will be able to build a relationship with them, better understand their needs, and get valuable feedback about what works on your platform and what doesn't.

---

78   www.sharetribe.com/booklinks, #74
79   www.sharetribe.com/booklinks, #75

Communicate buyer potential

Since customers have not yet found your platform, you need to convince your providers that they will eventually come. There are several ways to do this.

In an ideal world, you already have an existing community of potential customers. It can be a popular Instagram account, a mailing list, a popular blog, or a Facebook group. You should tell your providers that they will get instant access to this existing customer base if they sign up. Some marketplaces start by building the community first[80], then develop the marketplace business around it.

If you do not have such a community, you can try to find partners who can give you access to one. If you are creating a marketplace for fashion, you could start by contacting five popular fashion bloggers and offering to partner with them by giving them and their readers discounts in exchange for visibility. With these agreements in place, you can then mention to your providers that their products will be mentioned in these blogs.

Another example is a marketplace for tutors. In this case, you could try to partner with universities. Telling your potential tutor candidates that their offerings will be sent to the mailing lists of the five biggest universities of the country is a major selling point.

Create a single player mode

Finally, yet another way to attract providers is by creating an offering that provides value even with no customers at all. This is often called a single player mode[81] of two-sided platforms.

Using a marketplace for hairdressers as an example, the initial value proposition could be a Software-as-a-Service tool that can be used to manage the hairdressers' bookings, invoicing and accounting. It would be an easy way

---

80   www.sharetribe.com/booklinks, #76
81   www.sharetribe.com/booklinks, #77

for them to get an online presence, allowing them to direct their potential customers to your platform for booking and payments. This is what Finnish platform Timma did to build its original provider base. Another example from a different industry is Peek, a marketplace for experiences, which started with their Peek Pro offering. Additional benefit of these single player tools is that you can often sell them to the providers on a SaaS model and get initial revenue before having a single customer. Of course, putting on a price tag can increases the challenge in convincing the providers to sign up.

Another commonly used single player mode strategy is to find a way to offer your providers more visibility without building the marketplace component yourself. This can be done, as an example, by leveraging existing marketplaces. Thumbtack started by offering a tool for professionals to easily post their Thumbtack profiles to Craigslist. As CEO Marco Zappacosta explains:

> – *Independent pros were already using Craigslist—we simply helped them better show off the quality of their their work and highlight their online reputation.*[82]

In many service industries, this type of single player offering is compelling enough to get the providers to sign up—even without the additional benefit of gaining more customers through the marketplace model. Once you have enough providers, you can start attracting customers and gradually switch the focus towards a marketplace.

How to "fake" supply

In some situations, getting enough providers on board in the early days requires a lot of manual work. Before investing the time and money to go through with it, you might want to validate your concept with customers. In these cases, "faking" your supply—creating the supply in a way that is different from the marketplace model you eventually aim for—can be a good choice.

---

82   www.sharetribe.com/booklinks, #78

Create the initial inventory yourself

In the early days of your marketplace, if it is in any way possible, it might make sense for you to act as a provider yourself.

Morgan Brown, former head of growth at knowledge marketplace Growthackers.com, writes about their strategy:

> – *One way we supply hack is with our growth studies of different companies. It's our own supply engine of high-quality growth content.*[83]

If you are building a marketplace for used DVDs and have a large collection yourself, creating the initial supply by listing your own stuff is a no-brainer. You could also ask your friends and family to list—they might not be part of your eventual target group, but since they know you, they might be willing to help you out. Of course, this approach will not take scale well beyond the initial stages.

Pay for the inventory

If you have capital at your disposal, one way to make sure your marketplace has enough supply is to pay for the inventory[84]. This is what Uber did in the beginning: when they launched in Seattle, they paid town car drivers to idle[85]. Only once they had enough customers did they switch to paying a commission.

In some cases, you might be able to pay for inventory without risking big losses. Steve Sammartino used a clever approach when building his rental marketplace Rentoid. As he explains in a blog post[86], he would go through major department store catalogs, pick all the items that were suitable for renting, and list them on his site. When somebody rented an item, he went out and bought it. After renting the item, he would sell it on eBay for around 80%

83   www.sharetribe.com/booklinks, #79
84   www.sharetribe.com/booklinks, #80
85   www.sharetribe.com/booklinks, #81
86   www.sharetribe.com/booklinks, #82

of the original price. Using this method, he was able to get transactions on his site without losing money by holding a big inventory.

Aggregate existing inventory

Affiliate networks are one way to pre-fill your marketplace with inventory from other websites. Vacation rental marketplace Dwellable, later acquired by HomeAway, used this strategy in their early days. Udemy, a marketplace for online courses, did the same: they searched for courses legally available under a creative commons license and quickly grew their inventory to 5000 courses[87]. Thumbtack went even further, creating a massive web crawler[88] to find professional service providers.

The benefit of this approach is that you can reach massive scale without spending money. However, as Wertz and Kingyens point out in their guide, you should be cautious with this approach since it has two major problems:

– *First, while you may have a lot of inventory, none of it will be unique. Why should buyers come to your site instead of the other sites you're pulling inventory from? The second problem is that when you aggregate existing inventory, you run the risk of becoming a cross-platform utility rather than your own marketplace with lots of highly engaged users.*[89]

How much supply is needed?

Once you have enough initial supply, you can launch your marketplace to your first customers. We're going to cover strategies for the launch in the next chapter. Before we do that, we must first ask an important question: how much supply is enough?

The answer is that it largely depends on the type of marketplace, and namely on how many customers one provider can serve. This varies a lot. One way to

---

87   www.sharetribe.com/booklinks, #83
88   www.sharetribe.com/booklinks, #78
89   www.sharetribe.com/booklinks, #21

measure it is the ratio of transactions per customer (TPC) to transactions per provider (TPP). Venture Capitalist Willy Braun notes[90] how much these can vary in different marketplaces with three examples:

AirBnb: TPC/TPP = 1/70

Uber: TPC/TPP = 1/50

eBay: TPC/TPP = 1/5

On Airbnb, a customer might only travel once or twice a year, while the provider might constantly keep hosting new people. With Uber, the customer rides more frequently, but a provider can also serve a large number of customers every day. On eBay, people selling used stuff will run out of stuff to sell eventually, so there's a limit to how many customers they can serve.

What we learn from this equation is that if you're building a marketplace for selling pre-owned items, the initial amount of providers needs to be quite large to satisfy the needs of the customers—preferably more than a hundred. Meanwhile, if you're focusing on a highly specific local service, having just 5 or 10 providers could already satisfy the needs of your initial customer base.

How to build supply for a personal trainer marketplace

Let us put what we have learned to use with the case study from our previous chapters: a personal trainer marketplace.

After some research, you find there are no other marketplaces for personal trainers in your area. This means you cannot use them to find supply. However, as trainers are professional service providers, finding them is easy with business directories. You also contact local gyms, which act as "offline aggregators" for trainers. You manage to get a local gym to advertise your platform to all the 30 trainers they are affiliated with. You now have your initial list of trainers to contact.

---

90   www.sharetribe.com/booklinks, #84

You also strike a partnership with a local fitness blogger who gets excited about your concept. You offer her and her readership their first booking for free. You mention this partnership when you contact the trainers for the first time with a cold email. Since most of them know the blogger, it makes your platform more appealing to them as they want to associate themselves with the blogger's brand.

You decide to make your marketplace exclusive: only 50 trainers will be accepted in the beginning. You figure 50 is a big enough number for your launch. You interview and vet each trainer carefully, helping them create their listings to make sure the quality is good enough. You also ask each trainer if they know others who might be interested in your platform as well.

You also realize that many of the trainers don't have a web presence. This lets you offer a single player mode for them as well: a personal profile page with a description of their services, photos and videos, and a calendar that lets customers schedule an appointment and pay for it immediately. Many of your trainers use this option and start using their profile page as their online presence, directing their existing customers to it for booking.

Summary

By now, you should have an understanding of why it is important to first focus on one of the two sides of your marketplace. Typically, the better option is to start with your providers, building the initial supply before you open your platform to customers.

One good option for finding the first providers is to contact people who are already active in other marketplaces. If this is not a viable option, find the blogs, forums or other online communities where your target audience hangs out. Offline communities can also be effective initial sources. If you are dealing with professional service providers, you might also be able to find them on Google or online business directories.

You might need some creativity to convince your providers to list on a site with no customers. A good approach is to focus on quality and make the marketplace exclusive. If the providers are already active on other marketplaces, you need to highlight the benefits of your platform compared to the existing solutions. You should also communicate why you are able to bring them new customers, and, if possible, offer them a way to benefit from your platform even when there are no customers.

If you are unable to initially create a network of providers, you can "fake" supply by creating it yourself, paying for it, or aggregating existing supply from other online destinations.

If everything goes well, your platform is now ready to start taking on customers. In the next chapter, we're going to discuss how to facilitate your first transactions.

12

How to launch your marketplace

In the previous chapter, we learned how to seed your marketplace with supply. Your platform is now ready for its first customers.

It is time to put your marketplace to its first true test: can you facilitate transactions between your customers and providers? This will determine whether your marketplace actually provides value to its users.

As we stressed earlier, reaching high liquidity is crucial. High liquidity for customers is more important than having a large customer base. In other words, it is better to have fewer customers who have their needs met rather than a large group who do not. Similarly to when you were building supply, you should focus on quality over quantity when acquiring your first customers.

Most marketplaces are demand-constrained. This means that their core challenge lies in finding enough customers. Your team will likely spend most of their time tackling this challenge.

In this chapter, we are going to discuss different strategies for building your initial customer base and facilitating transactions between them and your providers.

How to find customers before launching

While your providers should be the first ones to get access to your platform, this does not mean you shouldn't be talking to your potential customers from the very beginning. Creating a simple email list to collect subscribers is a good idea.

This strategy worked well for the graphic design marketplace Creative Market. As co-founder Aaron Epstein explains[91], they set up a simple landing page to collect email addresses a few months before they actually opened up the marketplace. They even used the initial list to convince providers to join by telling them they already had plenty of interested people.

How should such a list be built? Simply setting up a landing page with a signup form is not enough. To get people to actually visit the site, you need to do some initial marketing. The strategies for finding your first customers are very similar to the ones for finding your first providers. You first need to understand who your potential early adopter customers are, and where they hang out—both online and offline. You can then think of the best ways to reach out to them. We will cover the most common strategies here.

Tap into existing communities

Your target customers may already be using a Facebook group or bulletin board to communicate. You should join the group and start participating in the discussions. Gradually, you can start mentioning your marketplace concept and asking for feedback. If you manage to attract some interest, direct them to your landing page to sign up for your email list.

For many marketplaces, university students are good initial target audiences. Student groups already have existing communication channels that you may be able to tap into.

When Juho was launching a marketplace for the students of University of Helsinki in 2012, he contacted each student association separately and pitched them to advertise the site on their mailing lists. As a result, the marketplace got lots of initial traction, which enabled the marketplace to become liquid.

---

91   www.sharetribe.com/booklinks, #85

Another similar campus launch was for the Aalto University marketplace in 2009. Juho managed to make signing up to the marketplace an exercise for a computer science 101 class that was mandatory for all freshmen. This was the only marketing effort that was required to get the site going. We encourage you to try to be creative when thinking about what channels you could use—you might find some surprising opportunities.

You should also think about who the major influencers of your target customers are. Are the influencers active bloggers? Contact them and try to make them your early ambassadors. This strategy worked well for Chicfy, a Spanish peer-to-peer marketplace that lets girls buy and sell fashion. They convinced ten well-known fashion bloggers to become their first providers and advertise the site to their audiences.

In some cases, your target audience might convene offline instead of online. You need to go where the audience is. Perhaps they host a monthly meetup, in which case you should attend with flyers in hand. The offline approach does not scale very well but gives you the opportunity to meet people face to face, which can turn them into dedicated supporters. As Airbnb's CEO Brian Chesky notes[92], it is way more important to find 100 people that love your service than a million people who think it's OK.

Airbnb has used the offline strategy efficiently whenever they move to a new city. Rebecca Rosenfelt, Product Manager at Airbnb, explains[93] how they would build teams of two or three people in each city and start talking to the community. They held parties, attended local events, and distributed flyers.

Start building your own community

If no existing community is available, you can start building your own. Again, it is important to understand who your target customers are and how they spend their days. There are many ways to build a community: by creating

92   www.sharetribe.com/booklinks, #86
93   www.sharetribe.com/booklinks, #87

a blog, being an active presence on social media sites, starting a forum, hosting offline meetups or events, or a mix of all of these.

A typical way to build a community is to create relevant content for your target audience and allow them to interact with it. This strategy is often referred to as content marketing.

The most common way to get started is with a blog. A good rule of thumb is that your content should aim to solve the same problem for your users as your product[94].

For example, if you are building a marketplace for gardening professionals, you could attract customers with a free gardening tips blog. The blog should be accompanied with a call to action to subscribe to your mailing list. You can also include a comments section to start building a community of engaged readers around your blog. If you wish to take a deeper dive to content marketing, we recommend Moz's *Beginner's Guide to Content Marketing*[95].

There are several ways to find an audience for your blog. One is to optimize the content so that people searching for the topic will find you through search engines. This is called search engine optimization (SEO). For getting started with SEO, check out Moz's *Beginner's Guide to SEO*[96].

Another way to spread your content is via social media. Whenever someone reads an article, you could encourage them to share it on their networks by adding share buttons at the end of the article.

A third way is to contact other bloggers and influencers in the same field: add comments to their blog posts, ask their opinion of your content, or offer to do guest posts on their blog. When you engage with their content, they will start engaging with yours.

For certain audiences, a blog might not be the best option. For instance, if you are targeting teenagers, you might need to go where they are. Today, that

---

94   www.sharetribe.com/boolinks, #88
95   www.sharetribe.com/booklinks, #89
96   www.sharetribe.com/booklinks, #90

might mean Snapchat or Instagram. Tomorrow, it probably means something different.

Starting a local Meetup group can also be a good way to build your initial community. This is likely the way to find your most loyal supporters, who will in turn refer your site to all their friends.

After you have seeded your marketplace and built the initial list of interested customers, you should be ready to let the first ones in—in other words, be ready to launch. In reality, there are two separate launches: the launch of your product and a marketing launch.

How to do a product launch

It's common for entrepreneurs to focus on their "launch date" and feel that it is really important to launch with a bang. However, this is not always the case. As Lean startup guru Eric Ries writes:

> – *Here's a common question I get from startups, especially in the early stages: when should we launch? My answer is almost always the same: don't.*[97]

As Ries explains, while there are some benefits to a big marketing launch, it can result in more problems than upside, especially if you have not yet validated your concept thoroughly. Your positioning might be off, and you end up spending time and money acquiring a large number of the wrong customers. Or, if your transaction flow is not yet optimal, your providers might become disappointed when they are not making enough sales.

Instead of big-bang launch, Ries gives a simple but important tip:

> – *Don't combine your product launch with a marketing launch. Instead, do your product launch first.*

What this means is that your marketplace should be open to the public for some time before you start promoting it widely.

---

97   www.sharetribe.com/booklinks, #91

A good way to do a product launch is to open up your marketplace platform, but only tell a small group of people about it. You should pick the most enthusiastic early adopters from your mailing list. Like with your first providers, you can play the exclusivity card here as well: tell the people that they are among the selected few that get to test your platform.

You can also offer a discount and ask for feedback in return. Be sure to communicate your marketing launch strategy to your providers so they don't spread the word about your marketplace before the time is right.

Now that you have the first users on your marketplace, it is the right time to calculate your liquidity rate. Simon Rothman estimates you should aim for a conversion rate of 30-60%.[98]

If 50 people to visit your site, but there are no transactions, you should contact those 50 people (which is why it is important to know who they are) and ask why they did not order anything. Was it because they did not understand what the site was for? Look into the way you are communicating your value proposition (see chapter eight). Was it because nothing they wanted was on offer? You need more supply (see chapter eleven) before you launch to a larger audience. Was finding what they were looking for too difficult? You might need to rethink the way your search & discovery process works (see chapter nine). Or perhaps they found something they wanted but did not complete a transaction for one reason or another, in which case you may need to make changes to your transaction flow (see chapter ten). After you have made changes, bring more people on board and see if the changes made a difference.

This approach may seem slow, but it is designed to reduce waste. As Rothman and Andrei Hagiu explain:

– *Marketplace entrepreneurs should resist the temptation to accelerate growth before figuring out an optimal supply-demand fit—that is, when buyers are as happy to purchase the products or services as*

---

98   www.sharetribe.com/booklinks, #60

providers are to supply them. This may mean waiting much longer than conventional companies do to scale a new offering.[99]

When you have finally validated that your platform is working well enough and your liquidity numbers are promising, it is time to get as much attention as possible with a marketing launch. This launch should be used to build initial momentum and attract a large group of users in one go. As Benjamin Edelman notes in his excellent essay "How to Launch Your Digital Platform"[100], a successful launch can significantly help in reaching critical scale.

How to do a marketing launch

The typical goal of a marketplace's marketing launch is to get customers (and providers) from your target segment to join and facilitate as many transactions as possible during the first days after the launch.

The most obvious option is to simply use the email list you built before launching. Creative Market, which we mentioned above, relied solely on this strategy when launching. They had managed to build a list of more than 70,000 potential buyers and 200 top sellers[101]. On their launch date, they simply sent an email to this list. Within 24 hours, they had made $3,000 in sales.

However, there are several other channels that can be used to get your marketing message across. They can be used to complement the email list option. The most common channels are listed below.

Press

When people think about a marketing launch, their first thought often goes to the press. While the press can be helpful, it is only one of many options. As Ries points out[102], you need to make sure you are getting the right press. Do your customers read TechCrunch? If not, it is probably not the right place

99   www.sharetribe.com/booklinks, #22
100   www.sharetribe.com/booklinks, #92
101   www.sharetribe.com/booklinks, #85
102   www.sharetribe.com/booklinks, #91

to launch—unless the main motivation for doing a press launch is to attract investors, but that's a whole different story.

The key to getting press is quite simple: you need to have a good story and pitch it to the right journalists—the ones who write for your specific target audience. The concept of your marketplace might in itself be good enough for a story, but in other cases, you might need to build the story. A good idea is to somehow tie your story to a recent newsworthy event that is interesting to journalists and offer a unique angle on it.

There are many strategies for getting press coverage. Instead of going through all of them here, we encourage you to start from Onstartups.com's excellent article "How to get media coverage for your startup: a complete guide"[103].

Influencers

Another way to do a marketing launch is to use the network of a "marquee contributor": an influencer your customers trust. As Edelman notes, to ensure a successful launch, you need to build enough credibility with your customers. This strategy helps you do exactly that.

Chicfy, which we discussed above, used this approach on their launch date by making use of the 10 bloggers they had acquired as providers. All these bloggers told their audiences about the launch.

The launch yielded good results for Chicfy: more than 16,000 visits to their site, over 1500 new users (including 600 new providers), and, most importantly, thousands of clothes were sold within the first few days. This success helped them establish their position as one of the most well known peer-to-peer marketplaces in Spain.

If you're planning on using this strategy, we recommend David Ly Khim's article:"A step-by-step guide to building lasting relationships with

---

103   www.sharetribe.com/booklinks, #92

influencers"[104], for a good overview of the different strategies for finding influencers and getting them on board.

Online communities

A third channel is to use online communities that are specifically dedicated to launching. The most widely known example of such a channel is Product Hunt, which aggregates new interesting products and allows users to vote for them. Getting featured in Product Hunt can bring you lots of attention for very little effort. This is what happened to Studiotime, the "Airbnb for record studios". In a matter of hours, more than 1000 users signed up for the site[105].

Getting featured on Product Hunt is notoriously hard nowadays with so much competition. As your chances are uncertain, you probably should not have Product Hunt as your only launch channel. Still, if you expect your target audience to be among Product Hunt users, it is worth trying. You can check out Justin Jackson's "The Product Hunt Handbook"[106], which is solely about the art of getting featured.

Which channel to pick

It is possible to use all these channels simultaneously for your launch. Whether that makes sense depends on your resources. Just like in all the other areas, having focus and favoring quality over quantity is important here as well. It is better to focus on one channel and do it well rather than fail in multiple channels at once.

Airbnb's Rosenfelt advises you to launch with all you've got[107]. Whenever they launch in a new city, they do several things at once: send press releases, hold parties, perform offline guerilla tactics. For example, when Airbnb opened their office in Barcelona in February of 2012, Brian Chesky and other members

104   www.sharetribe.com/booklinks, #94
105   www.sharetribe.com/studiotime.html
106   www.sharetribe.com/booklinks, #95
107   www.sharetribe.com/booklinks, #87

from the team came to the city to host a launching party with hundreds of Airbnb hosts and other members. Do note that Airbnb already had lots of resources at this time, meaning they could afford to do multiple channels at once and do them well.

Timing matters

If you can launch your platform at a time when there's particularly high demand for the services you provide, great. This typically means there are some constraints on the supply side, which means your initial providers will be in high demand. Airbnb used this strategy[108] to time their launches in new cities.

Some marketplaces are seasonal. If you want to create a marketplace for renting out swimming pools in France, the right timing is everything because there's only demand during a certain season. Swimmy launched their platform just before the summer holiday season. This also helped them a lot with press, as during the summertime journalists are often looking for "lighter" stories that fit the summer mood, and they had a perfect story for people looking to organize a pool party.

What to do if the marketing launch fails

So you launched and nobody came? Fear not. It's not the end of the world. As Airbnb's Chesky famously said:

– If you launch and no one notices, launch again. We launched 3 times.[109]

In fact, a bigger failure is a "successful" marketing launch with the wrong positioning. You end up positioning your product in a way that requires lots of time and money to correct. Eric Ries had such an experience with his startup IMVU:

---

108   www.sharetribe.com/booklinks, #96
109   www.sharetribe.com/booklinks, #97

— We did some early press (in Wired, no less) for IMVU that called us the next generation of IM and compared us positively to AOL. At the time, we thought that was great. Now, I look back and cringe. Being compared to AOL isn't so great these days, and IM is considered a pretty weak form of socializing. When we finally launched for real, we had to compensate for that early blunder.[110]

As we discussed above, this is an issue you can avoid by separating your product launch from your marketing launch, and testing your concept rigorously before opening it up to larger audiences.

How to launch your personal trainer marketplace

It is time to put what we have learned in this chapter to use and design a launch strategy for the personal trainer marketplace that we have been using as an example in previous chapters.

We previously identified your early adopter customers as "wealthy stay-at-home moms between the ages of 30 and 50". You also defined your main value proposition to them as "the easiest way to get fit". The problem you are solving for them is overcoming the difficulty in getting started.

This problem can be solved with a marketplace, but it can also be solved with a blog. Thus, you start a blog that offers easy training tips for people who want to get fit. You identify the most important keywords and target your posts accordingly. You also work together with the fitness blogger you struck a partnership with (in chapter eleven) by offering to write a guest post on her blog, and ask her to write one for you as well. On your blog, you create a call to action for people to subscribe to your mailing list.

After you have onboarded the first trainers and gained some initial traction with your blog, it is time to launch the product to a small number of customers. You decide to send an email to 100 people on your email list and tell them they are getting exclusive access to the early beta of your site. You give them all a

---

110   www.sharetribe.com/booklinks, #91

personal access code to the site, and promise them a 50% discount on their first booking.

You closely track how many of these people end up visiting your site and make bookings. If you do not get enough visitors—you probably want to have at least a few hundred to get statistically significant results—you email more people until you have a sufficient number. You contact some of them to ask them about their experience. Based on the insights from these discussions, you make a few adjustments to your filters and change the wording of your landing page slightly.

After some initial testing, you conclude that the initial traction seems promising: every third visitor ends up making a booking on your site. You decide it is time to release the site to a bigger audience.

As you are only launching in one city, you do not really care about reaching national newspapers. Since your audience is not that interested in tech or startups, you pass tech blogs. Product Hunt is also not relevant for you.

Instead, you focus solely on the biggest newspaper in your city. You figure your target audience still reads paper magazines, making it an effective way to get their attention. As a bonus, the paper has an online version as well. Since a story about a marketplace for personal trainers is not an interesting enough story as such, you dig up some statistics that show how much healthier people who use personal trainers are, and how big an impact using such services can have on one's life. You accompany the story with a simple infographic. You manage to pitch this story to a reporter who you know through a friend, and they promise to write a story where your site is also mentioned.

You also take advantage of the partnership you made (in chapter eleven) with a local gym. Together, you decide that everyone who books one of the gym's trainers through the site gets a 50% discount off their first booking, and the provider does not have to pay your fees from that booking. The gym also promises to send an email newsletter about your launch to its members and put up your poster on their notice board. You strike a similar deal with your fitness blogger partner.

On the launch date, the following things happen:

- You send an email to everyone on your mailing list, notifying them about the launch.
- The gym sends a newsletter about your launch.
- The local newspaper publishes the article.
- Your blogger partner publishes a post about your launch and tweets about it.
- You share all this through your social media channels and ask your friends and team members to do the same.

Combined, these activities are enough to bring you initial liquidity. Your marketplace now has a small but dedicated group of early users. Congratulations, you're off to a good start!

However, this is just the beginning. You now need to figure out how to scale.

Summary

In this chapter, you learned how to find your initial customers, get them to use your product, and how to do a bigger marketing launch.

The key to building your initial customer base is to start building an email list before you launch. You will find people either by tapping into existing communities or creating your own.

You should not launch in one go with a big bang. Instead, let a small group of customers use your marketplace at first, and test your process with them. Only when you are confident your concept is working well should you move on to a bigger marketing launch.

In addition to the email list, there are several channels you can utilize during the launch. Some of the common ones include press, influencers, and online communities like Product Hunt.

13

How to grow your marketplace

In the previous chapter, we covered marketplace launch strategies and ways to get initial traction. With these tips, you were able to launch successfully and now have a stable initial user base. Transactions are flowing in. However, the size of your user base is still small. It's time to grow your marketplace.

As Boris Wertz and Angela Tran Kingyens explain in their marketplace handbook[111], the key to growing a marketplace is to reach a virtuous cycle: high-quality providers bring in more customers, and the growing customer base in turn attracts more providers. In this chapter, we are going to discuss how to attain this cycle.

How fast should a marketplace grow?

Before we dive into growth tactics, we first need to talk about growth itself. Understanding what kind of growth to expect is important in order to set realistic expectations. In general, building marketplace businesses takes more time than other online businesses. Wertz and Tran Kingyens urge marketplace founders to be patient:

— *With a typical SaaS or e-commerce startup, you probably should reassess your market or model if you don't see signs of traction after*

---

111   www.sharetribe.com/booklinks, #21

six to nine months. However, this timetable is way too accelerated for marketplaces. Considering you need to establish both buyer and seller communities, you will need more time to prove your business. It can take three years for a marketplace to get going.

As startup guru Paul Graham writes, the most common reason for startup companies to die is a loss of faith in their business[112]. This is especially common for marketplaces, where it may seem like the business is not going anywhere for a long time. It took 4 years before Airbnb really took off[113].

Don't be one of the founders who gives up too soon. Be patient. Constantly try new things, but don't give up. You'll get there eventually.

Growing too fast may actually kill a marketplace business. As Andrei Hagiu and Simon Rothman write in their excellent essay, Network Effects Aren't Enough: "Growing too early amplifies flaws in the business model, making them harder to fix." Figuring out the optimal revenue stream that extracts enough value—but not too much—from your transactions can only be done through trial and error. If you scale too fast without finding this optimal model, it can lead to a breakdown of your business.[114]

However, things should be moving forward constantly. You should see some sort of improvement every month: more provider signups, more transactions, improved liquidity. If this is not happening despite your continuous efforts, changes need to be made. This is where growth tactics come in.

How to find the right growth channel

Multiple growth strategies exist for all types of marketplaces. The key is to quickly test different channels to figure out which ones work, and focus on those channels.

Gabriel Weinberg and Justin Mares provide a useful framework for this process in their book Traction: How Any Startup Can Achieve Explosive

---

112   www.sharetribe.com/booklinks, #98
113   www.sharetribe.com/booklinks, #99
114   www.sharetribe.com/booklinks, #22

Customer Growth[115]. The framework is called Bullseye[116]. It is based on a simple method:

1. Start by brainstorming potential growth ideas.
2. Select the most promising ones, and perform quick tests with each, all in parallel. Each test should last no more than a month.
3. Once the tests are done, select the channel that worked the best and focus on it until it no longer "moves the needle".

Weinberg and Mares explain that in order for a channel to "move the needle", it should be moving you closer to your growth target at a fast enough pace. Different channels work well at different stages. One channel can be perfect for reaching 1000 monthly transactions, but might not help when your goal is to reach 100,000 transactions per month. When a channel no longer has the desired effect, you need to find a new channel.

Weinberg and Mares identified the 19 most common channels[117] that any business can use to get traction. You may notice that there is some overlap between the channels, and they often work best when combined together. We will only cover the channels that are most commonly used by successful marketplaces in this chapter, but it is a good idea to keep all of them in mind in case you come up with ways to leverage them. We will not go very deeply into the channels in this book, but you can read more in-depth articles about them on the Marketplace Academy.

Viral marketing

Viral marketing means growing your user base by encouraging your users to bring in new customers. It is a key acquisition channel for many marketplaces since it is a requirement for the virtuous cycle that Wertz and Tran Kingyens talk about. It is also a scalable method—the effect increases as your user base

---

115   www.sharetribe.com/booklinks, #100
116   www.sharetribe.com/booklinks, #101
117   www.sharetribe.com/booklinks, #102

grows without requiring more work from you. To make your marketplace viral, you need to give your users an incentive to invite others.

The best incentive depends on the nature of your marketplace. In many cases, an online marketplace may be the first time a professional provider gets an online presence. In these situations, educating providers on how to market their offering outside your marketplace[118] is a solid strategy. After all, helping your providers find customers is great not just for them, but for the marketplace as well. As an example, Etsy created a seller handbook[119] that offers great advice on how to do marketing. In an ideal scenario, your providers become your marketing team.

Customers do not have similar intrinsic incentives to bring on other customers, which is why you need to create an incentive. A common way to create a "viral loop" is to offer monetary compensation for referrals. Airbnb makes use of this strategy; they offer discounts for customers that bring new guests and hosts onboard.

It is also possible to combine these two viral strategies. For example, Udemy allows instructors to keep a bigger portion of each sale[120] if they handle promotion of their courses themselves.

Our experience is that people who are new to marketplaces tend to overestimate its viral growth potential. Unlike social networks, marketplaces tend not to be viral by nature. Social networks grow because people need their friends or colleagues to be there to interact with them. In marketplaces, people mostly interact with strangers, so the incentives for getting acquaintances onboard don't exist. Because of this, you generally need to rely on other strategies as well.

---

118   www.sharetribe.com/booklinks, #103
119   www.sharetribe.com/booklinks, #104
120   www.sharetribe.com/booklinks, #105

Search engine optimization

Search engine optimization (SEO) is the process of improving your rank in search engine results to help more people find your site. Instead of promoting yourself actively to potential customers, you make yourself easy to find for those who are looking for the products or services on your marketplace.

For a marketplace, most of the SEO work lies on the shoulders of the providers. The key is—again—to educate them about best practices. Etsy does a great job here as well, offering a comprehensive guide for its sellers on how to get found.

There are certain things that a marketplace can and should do to help with SEO. Tradesy, a marketplace for pre-owned high-quality fashion, gets a significant amount of sales from unpaid search traffic[121], largely because it has structured its listings in a way that makes it easy for search engines to crawl the marketplace. Course Hero, a marketplace for study resources, uses a similar strategy effectively.

Besides providing the right structure for search engines to crawl, another important factor is whether or not your marketplace platform generates the necessary metadata for each page. In addition to visible aspects like the page title, it also includes "invisible" things in each page's source code, such as a description and social media images. When evaluating different marketplace platforms, make sure that the platform handles these in an adequate manner.

For additional SEO tips, we recommend "The Beginner's Guide to SEO"[122] by Moz and the "SEO Guide for Marketplaces and eCommerce Sites"[123] from KissMetrics.

---

121   www.sharetribe.com/booklinks, #106
122   www.sharetribe.com/booklinks, #90
123   www.sharetribe.com/booklinks, #107

Content marketing

As we discussed in the previous chapter, content marketing is a good way to start building your initial customer base. Your content can also be used to help you grow in three ways.

First, it improves your search engine ranking (SEO). People will stumble across your content when they search for your marketplace's niche, through which they will discover your marketplace.

Second, quality content gets shared on social media. If you manage to create an engaging piece of content, it might be seen by millions of readers with little or no promotion. However, you shouldn't rely too much on this effect as it takes a great deal of luck to create such a phenomenon.

Third, your content can help your providers improve their offering. Etsy's Seller handbook, which we discussed above, is a great example of content marketing. It helps Etsy sellers sell more effectively, but new sellers also discover Etsy directly through the handbook.

Paying for traffic

If you have capital at your disposal, it can be used to buy growth. The most common way to do it is through Search Engine Marketing, i.e. displaying ads on Google or other search engines based on the search keywords. Social Media Marketing (promoted content on sites like Facebook and Twitter) or banner ads are other popular forms of paid advertising.

The challenge with paid ads is that you need to be sure the return on your investment is positive. You need to get back more money than what you are spending on ads. With marketplaces, calculating the return is tricky since you cannot really be sure how much a user is worth. A new user may become a provider that generates thousands of transactions, or they may never take part in a single transaction.

Another challenge for paid marketing is competition. Since ads are generally bought auction-style—with companies bidding for placement—advertising for popular search terms on Google can become very expensive. A good way to circumvent this is to try to find the keywords that have a relatively large search volume but are not being advertised on. Google also gives a "discount" for ads that are relevant to whatever is being searched for. Having high-quality content and good SEO can pay off in the form of reduced ad prices.

In most cases, paid ads are not suitable as the main acquisition channel for early-stage marketplaces due to cost. The situation may be different if you have deep pockets and are in a "winner takes it all" market where you need to grab market share before your competitors. Uber executed this strategy effectively in many cities[124]—but only after they had perfected their base offering.

However, this does not mean early stage marketplaces should not take advantage of paid ads. They can be very useful in testing out marketing angles. For instance, if you believe you should focus your SEO and content marketing efforts on people who perform certain types of queries in Google, running a Google AdWords campaign is an easy way to test whether you should pay for the top position for certain keywords. You will see quickly how large the search volume is, how much ads for them cost, and how large a portion of people who click on your ad actually end up making a purchase.

Typically, paying for traffic is a good strategy for acquiring a new customer if you have a high average repeat purchase ratio (the likeliness of a user performing a new transaction after their initial purchase). Thus, you typically want to combine paid acquisition with email marketing.

Email marketing

There's a statistic that says, on average, attracting new customers costs 5 times as much as keeping an existing customer[125]. Marketplaces generally spend too much time acquiring new users instead of activating existing ones.

In the previous chapter, we discussed the importance of building an email list early on. This work should be continued after you launch. Email is the most effective way to reach your existing users and activate them on your

---

124   www.sharetribe.com/booklinks, #108
125   www.sharetribe.com/booklinks, #109

marketplace. The list should be used actively to send your users offers, lists of interesting new products or services on your marketplace, useful articles from your blog, and so on.

Etsy has done a great job keeping the people who make their first purchase active on the site. In 2014, a whopping 78 percent of its sales came from repeat customers. This is quite likely a key reason for why Etsy requires every buyer to become a user.

A good way to use the email list is to tell the stories of your successful customers. This strategy of creating social proof is vital in creating the virtuous cycle: as soon as someone is making a profit on your marketplace, others will become interested and more active, increasing the number of success stories. Udemy used this strategy heavily as soon as their instructors started making serious money.

Build a community

Many successful modern marketplaces succeed by building active communities around their offering. Airbnb specifically refers to itself as a community marketplace. Meanwhile, Etsy proclaims to be "more than a marketplace: we're a community." Both platforms want its users to engage with each other and spend time on their site—even when they do not intend to buy anything.

This is often a smart move since it builds retention: if your users feel like they are part of a community, they are less likely to jump ship to other marketplaces. Community-building is such an important topic for marketplace entrepreneurs that we have dedicated chapter 16 entirely to that topic.

Engineering as marketing

Sometimes, the best way to grow is to build new growth-oriented functionality into your product. The term "growth hacker", which is often used to describe digital marketers in general, was originally coined by growth specialist Andrew Chen—who headed supply growth at Uber—to mean a marketer that uses technical skills to foster growth.

As a case example, Chen used Airbnb's Craigslist integration[126]. We'll discuss it in more detail in the next section, where we take a closer look at how Airbnb used different channels at different phases of their growth.

Case study: Airbnb's growth story

Airbnb's growth story has been well documented by Morgan Brown in a GrowthHackers.com case study[127]. We encourage you to read it in its entirety, but will recap the essentials here.

In 2009, during Airbnb's early stages, they started by doing things that did not scale. The founders went to stay at a bunch of Airbnb apartments themselves to figure out why they were not getting more bookings. They identified low-quality photographs as the culprit and decided to invest time and money in taking better photos. This boosted initial growth.

The next bottleneck was supply. To combat this, Airbnb used email marketing and contacted people who were listing their apartments on Craigslist to explain the benefits of Airbnb. They used a rather sketchy and spammy strategy[128] for this, which we do not recommend. Instead of using fake emails, they could have simply sent the same emails from their own accounts. Nevertheless, it helped them get enough supply to reach the next level.

After getting more suppliers on board, the bottleneck switched back to demand. For this, they again turned to Craigslist, which had a large amount of potential customers visiting it every day. This time, they turned things around: instead of convincing Craigslist users to advertise their property on Airbnb, they urged hosts to post Airbnb ads on Craigslist. This was engineering as marketing. They built an integration that made it easy to advertise an Airbnb

126   www.sharetribe.com/booklinks, #110
127   www.sharetribe.com/booklinks, #111
128   www.sharetribe.com/booklinks, #112

listing on Craigslist directly from Airbnb's user interface. Andrew Chen explains how the process worked.

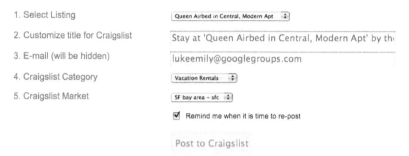

Post to Craigslist

Reach thousands of people, instantly by re-posting your Airbnb listing (photos, reviews, description) to Craigslist. Travelers will be redirected back to Airbnb to contact & book with you. For help, click here.

1. Select Listing   Queen Airbed in Central, Modern Apt

2. Customize title for Craigslist   Stay at 'Queen Airbed in Central, Modern Apt' by the

3. E-mail (will be hidden)   lukeemily@googlegroups.com

4. Craigslist Category   Vacation Rentals

5. Craigslist Market   SF bay area - sfc

☑ Remind me when it is time to re-post

Post to Craigslist

Screenshot of Airbnb's Craigslist integration.

At some point, Airbnb had exhausted Craigslist as a channel. They needed to build the viral engine that would feed itself. On average, each existing user should bring in more than one new user. To do that, they built a carefully designed referral program that created incentives for people to invite their friends. This process is documented in detail in the Airbnb Nerds blog[129]. With this setup in place, Airbnb managed to create the virtuous cycle Wertz and Tran Kingyens talk about.

Scaling beyond your initial niche

As we have discussed earlier, during the early stages of a marketplace, it is vital to focus on a narrow niche. However, if things go well, at some point you may capture such a large share of your initial niche market that there is no more room to grow. At that point, you need to start thinking about scaling beyond your initial focus.

---

129   www.sharetribe.com/booklinks, #113

Boris Wertz describes three strategies for moving from the niche to the masses[130]. The most obvious one is to add more categories. This worked well for Amazon, which started with just books, but today offers all types of products. Similarly, eBay started by focusing on specific categories, like Beanie Babies[131], before gradually expanding.

A good sign that it is time to expand is when you start seeing lots of items on your marketplace that do not have their own category. This is how Etsy expanded to crafting supplies.

Another strategy is to start catering to new audiences. Perhaps your platform first focuses only on university students, like Facebook did, and later expands to other demographics as well.

The third option is to keep the same focus but expand the size of the market itself. As Wertz explains, this worked well for Lululemon and Etsy: yoga is way bigger today than it was ten years ago, and the maker movement and enthusiasm towards arts & crafts have seen similar explosive growth. As an example of how to expand a market, Etsy started to educate aspiring entrepreneurs on how to become crafts sellers[132].

As you scale, you will face new types of problems. Umang Dua and Oisin Hanrahan started Handy as a marketplace for home cleaning services, and later expanded to other local service categories. They write about their scaling process, and how the challenges they face have changed tremendously[133]. The main issue with scaling is that while in the early days you can fix problems as they arise, putting out fires is no longer enough when you grow. You need to fix the underlying causes instead.

How can you deal with this challenge? How do you know which problems to prioritize? As Dua and Hanrahan recommend:

130   www.sharetribe.com/booklinks, #114
131   www.sharetribe.com/booklinks, #103
132   www.sharetribe.com/booklinks, #115
133   www.sharetribe.com/booklinks, #116

– The base level of the pyramid starts with trust—without trust nothing else matters. If your customers don't trust you, they won't use your service.

Building trust in your user community is the one most important thing for most marketplaces to achieve true scale. This is another topic that is important enough to be covered on its own in chapter 15.

How to grow your personal trainer marketplace

Let's jump back to our fictional personal trainer marketplace from previous chapters and put what we have learned into practice.

You already created a blog (see chapter twelve) as part of your launch strategy, and content marketing combined with email updates about new offers remains at the core of your marketing.

Your blog also improves your search engine ranking. You continue researching the most important keywords and write about those topics on your blog, and also frequently publish guest posts in other blogs. After a while, these new blog posts bring you free visibility for those search terms. You remember to direct blog readers directly to your marketplace. You test the impact of the best keywords with quick Google AdWords campaigns.

You decide to create a guide for your trainers on how to advertise their services online. It includes advice on how to create high-quality photos and videos, how to optimize their profile for search engines, and even how to buy paid ads. This allows you to outsource part of your marketing efforts to the trainers.

You approach all your trainers regularly to remind them to invite their customers to the marketplace. It makes sense for the trainers since your platform helps them with invoicing and scheduling. The more of their customers that use your site, the easier it is for the trainers. You decide to incentivize customers to invite new members with a special offer: for each new person that a customer gets on board, both the invitee and the existing customer get 50% off their next booking. This allows you to create a viral loop.

Summary

In this chapter, we discussed different strategies for growing your marketplace. While growth is important, marketplaces need more time to grow than traditional online businesses. You need to be patient and grow slowly in the beginning in order to validate and optimize your business.

When you are ready to scale, you should test different growth channels to find the one that works best for that growth stage, and focus on it until it is exhausted. It might make sense to use multiple channels in parallel as they can complement each other effectively. The most common marketplace growth channels are viral marketing, search engine optimization, content marketing, paid advertising, email marketing, community-building and engineering as marketing.

At a certain stage, it may be time to scale beyond your initial niche. This can be done by expanding your categories, your audience demographic, or the market itself. As you scale, the set of challenges you face will change, and you need to learn new ways to handle them.

Now that your marketplace is growing, how do you know whether it is successful or not?

14

How to measure your success: The key marketplace metrics

How do you know if your marketplace is successful? One might think that growing your user base and having transactions is enough. Things are, however, quite a bit more nuanced than that.

Before anything else, you need to define what success means to you. Do you want to build a global business or are you satisfied with a local one? In any case, in this chapter we assume that you want to generate at least enough revenue to become ramen profitable[134]—in other words, to reach the minimum amount of revenue to be able to support your team full-time.

To get to profitability, you need to be able to grow. You need to create a virtuous cycle where your customers are constantly bringing in more providers and providers are bringing in more customers.

To understand if things are moving in the right direction, there are certain metrics (or Key Performance Indicators, KPIs) you should follow rigorously, and take immediate action if they are pointing south. In this chapter, we will go over the most important KPIs for marketplace businesses.

---

134   www.sharetribe.com/booklinks, #117

Usage metrics

Usage metrics help you understand how many people visit your site and how they spend time on it. These metrics are not specific to marketplaces. Every website monitors the same basic metrics to track their growth. The three most important usage metrics are monthly active users, bounce rate and time spent on site.

Monthly Active Users (MAU)

A common way to track user activity is to measure *monthly active users*. Typically, this is done by counting the number of unique users who have visited your site at least once during a certain time period. If this number is not growing, it means you are either not attracting new users or you are losing old ones faster than you gain new ones. Either way, you are in trouble.

Bounce rate

Getting lots of visitors on your site is not very helpful if the visitors leave immediately without doing anything. Bounce rate measures the percentage of visitors who land on your site and leave right away ("bounce") rather than stay to engage with your site in some way. According to a recently published statistic, popular marketplaces like eBay, Amazon and Etsy have a bounce rate somewhere between 20% and 25%, while some less popular (and thus less successful) sites have significantly higher rates[135]. You should aim for a low rate as possible.

Time spent on site

If your users do not bounce, you can start measuring how much time they spend on your site. Marketplaces differ from social media sites with regards to this metric: with social media, the goal is to have people spend as much time as

---

135   www.sharetribe.com/booklinks, #118

possible on the site, while with marketplaces, this may not be desirable. Long times might be an indicator that users cannot find what they are looking for.

Nevertheless, comparison data clearly shows that the most successful marketplaces also have the highest time spent on site figures. If your users spend time browsing your site, it is quite likely they also end up buying more.

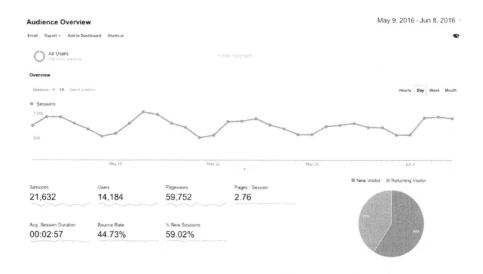

Google Analytics is a good free tool for measuring usage metrics

These three metrics are not only interesting to you. If your providers are savvy, they will ask about them as well. Today, providers can use comparison websites to choose a marketplace in which to sell their products or services. MAU, bounce rate and time spent on site are three numbers they will use to compare you to others.

For social media sites, usage metrics are often the most important metrics—and, in some cases, the only thing they focus on. For marketplaces, this is almost never the case. As we stated in chapter twelve (How to launch your marketplace), the goal of any marketplace should be to facilitate transactions between its users and achieve liquidity. Usage metrics do not tell you whether you are getting closer to that goal. Because of this, you should not focus on them too much; for many marketplaces, they can actually be vanity metrics[136].

We are now going to take a look at some marketplace-specific KPIs.

Transaction metrics

When you start looking at transaction-related metrics, it is tempting to focus on the number of transactions. However, just like with the number of users, this can be yet another vanity metric. The number of transactions is not really actionable: it does not tell you what you should change. To foster sustainable growth, we recommend focussing on these metrics instead: liquidity, provider-to-customer ratio, and repeat purchase ratio.

Liquidity

As we learned in chapter ten, every marketplace should strive for high liquidity, which is defined as "a reasonable expectation of selling something you list or finding what you are looking for." This dual nature of liquidity means you actually have two different figures to measure: provider liquidity and customer liquidity.

Liquidity is measured as a percentage. Sangeet Paul Choudary defines provider liquidity as "the percentage of listings that lead to transactions within a certain time period"[137]. In practice, provider liquidity is calculated a bit differently for different types of marketplaces. In retail, it's simply the amount of sales divided by current inventory, which is also often called the sell-through rate[138]. On Etsy, for instance, it is the total amount of sales over a certain time period divided by how many items the sellers had for sale in total during that same period. One month is a good time interval for this type of marketplace. On Airbnb, you want to measure liquidity daily: how large a proportion of rooms are booked each night. On Uber, you might need to

136   www.sharetribe.com/booklinks, #119
137   www.sharetribe.com/booklinks, #120
138   www.sharetribe.com/booklinks, #121

measure it hourly: how big a percentage of drivers that are on duty are driving a customer at any given hour.

Customer liquidity means the probability of a visit leading to a transaction. According to Simon Rothman, a good goal is between 30 and 60 percent (note: we assume this is not counting people who bounce). A simple but approximate way to measure this is to calculate how many visits you get on a given month, and how many transactions you get in the same period. Typically, most visits on your site are from potential customers, but, naturally, the figure is more accurate if you can filter out visits from your providers.

Provider-to-customer ratio

To better understand the nature of your marketplace's inner dynamics, another crucial metric to follow is provider-to-customer ratio (also called Buyer-to-Seller ratio[139]). We define this as the number of customers that one provider can serve. There is no single right ratio that all marketplaces should strive for. In some cases, the provider-to-customer ratio might be as low as 1:1 (one provider can serve only one customer—think real estate), while in others it may be as high as 1:10,000 (one provider can serve 10,000 customers—think stock photos). As we learned in chapter eleven, Airbnb's figure is 1:70, Uber's is 1:50, and eBay's is 1:5[140].

The more customers one provider can serve, the more you should focus on supply in the beginning. The math behind the reasoning is quite simple: when you are acquiring users by hand, acquiring a provider is more valuable than acquiring a customer since the provider will likely participate in more transactions.

However, if you have a high provider-to-customer ratio, you will eventually need to grow your customer base at a faster rate than your provider base in order to reach provider liquidity. This means that the biggest constraint to marketplace growth will eventually be demand.

---

139   www.sharetribe.com/booklinks, #122
140   www.sharetribe.com/booklinks, #123

Repeat purchase ratio

One more useful transaction metric is how big a percentage of your transactions are repeat purchases[141], i.e. from people who have already made purchases on your site. As we learned in the previous chapter, Etsy has mastered the art of repeat purchases with 78% of its sales coming from existing customers. Airbnb's repeat purchase ratio is 22%.

The higher the percentage, the more money you can afford to spend on acquiring new customers since a customer will likely make multiple transactions. Conversely, if repeat purchase are unlikely, you might run into trouble when trying to grow. This is what happened to NextMover[142], a "Lyft for moving help". Their initial customer base started growing nicely, but they realized people do not move very often, so repeat purchases were rare. Because of this, their customer acquisition costs (which we will talk about later) ballooned, and they had to pull the plug.

If your MAU is growing constantly and you have good liquidity on both the customer and the provider side, the dynamics of your marketplace are in good shape. However, this does not yet mean that you have a good business. It's not enough to be able to provide value to your users—you also need to capture some of that value to be financially sustainable. Next, we will look at the most important business KPIs for marketplaces.

Business metrics

Business metrics aim to answer questions related to your revenue, profitability, and customer acquisition. The three most important figures are gross merchandise volume, customer acquisition cost, and customer lifetime value

141   www.sharetribe.com/booklinks, #124
142   www.sharetribe.com/booklinks, #125

Gross Merchandise Volume (GMV)

To understand if your marketplace is a good business, you should start from the *Gross Merchandise Volume*. It means the total sales value of the products or services sold through your marketplace during a specific time period. If you want to only use one figure to measure the total growth of your marketplace, use this one instead of the number of users or products.

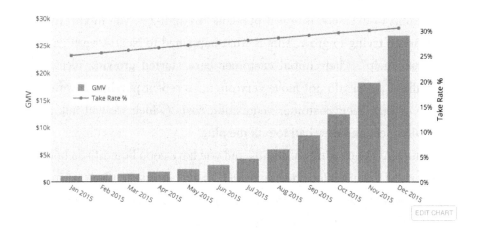

A graph to visualize GMV and take rate of a marketplace from plot.ly

However, while GMV is a good way to estimate the size of a marketplace business, it is not sufficient to understand the marketplace's health[143]. To calculate your total revenue, you need to multiply the GMV by your take rate (your commission from each transaction).

Customer Acquisition Cost (CAC)

Customer acquisition cost means the price you pay to acquire a new customer. In an ideal situation, this number is close to zero: each customer

---

143   www.sharetribe.com/booklinks, #122

refs at least one new potential customer to your site, and your audience grows organically, without you having to do anything.

Unfortunately, this is rarely the case. Even if you do not spend any money on marketing, you will likely need to spend more on support and community management as your user base grows. More often than not, you also want to accelerate growth with paid ad campaigns, where it is vital to understand how much money you are spending for each new customer.

Customer Lifetime Value (CLV)

Customer lifetime value means the total amount of revenue you expect to get from each customer. As a rule of thumb, CLV should be higher than CAC. If not, your growth is not sustainable. As Phil Hu notes, CLV can also help you determine an optimal provider-to-customer ratio for your marketplace[144].

Calculating an exact CLV can be tricky since it depends on how long you are able to retain a customer, how many repeat purchases you expect them to make, and the size of your average transaction.

However, it is still possible to have some sort of estimate for CLV[145], which is a great way to evaluate the viability of your business. For instance, if you divide the GMV by the amount of transactions per month, you get your average order value (AOV). Multiply this by the average amount of repeat purchases per customer to get CLV.

What should you do if your CAC is higher than CLV? It depends on the cause. To find the root cause of the problem, you need to understand your customer conversion funnel.

Customer conversion funnel

An important metric related to your transaction process is your customer conversion percentage: the proportion of new visitors that end up buying something on your site. The customer conversion funnel tracks the path that

---

144   www.sharetribe.com/booklinks, #123
145   www.sharetribe.com/booklinks, #126

new visitors take before making a purchase, usually consisting of several steps. If the prospective customer does not bounce, their first likely action is to search for a product or service or click on a product category. They might check multiple products, decide they are not the right ones, and return to search. At some point, they find what they are looking for and click the Buy button. As we learned in chapter ten on the transaction flow, even at this point it is not certain they will actually follow through with the purchase.

To understand where your biggest bottleneck is, you need to be able to measure your customer conversion funnel and see where most people drop off. You can then focus on fixing the bottleneck, and see how the changes impact the funnel.

Several different conclusions can be made from this data. If the number of visitors is low in general, you should do more customer acquisition (see chapters 12 and 13). If your bounce rate is high, it might be a sign that your customer acquisition strategy is not working, and you are acquiring the wrong type of people.

Alternatively, you might need to improve your landing page and refine your core value proposition (see chapter eight). If people do not bounce but they never end up visiting a listing or their searches do not return relevant results, you might have a customer liquidity issue. This means you should either get more providers on board (see chapter eleven) or narrow down your focus to get fewer but more relevant customers.

If you have the right products but the customer did not manage to find them, your problem lies in your discovery process (see chapter nine). If people visit many listings but do not continue to checkout, you might have an issue with the quality of supply (see chapter eleven) or the customers are trying to bypass your fees (see chapter four). If you notice that many people click the Buy button but do not follow through with the transaction, the problem is with your transaction flow (see chapter ten).

While studying the usage, transaction, and conversion numbers can take you a long way, there is a limit to what you can learn from these metrics. They only tell you what happened, but not why it happened. There is one final metric that you should not forget: user satisfaction. Next, we will talk about how to measure user satisfaction in a quantifiable way.

User satisfaction metrics

There are multiple ways to measure customer satisfaction. We will introduce two useful methods for marketplace businesses: Net Promoter Score (NPS) and the product/market fit survey.

Net Promoter Score (NPS)

If you are only using one metric to measure user satisfaction, we recommend Net Promoter Score. It was popularized by the 2003 Harvard Business Review article "The One Number You Need to Grow" by Frederick F. Reichheld[146], and is used widely today.

The score is obtained by asking the following question: "How likely is it that you would recommend [product] to a friend or colleague?" The answer is a number from 0 to 10. This question works well because if someone is likely to recommend your product, it means they are getting value from it themselves. This gives us more accurate satisfaction results than simply asking if your users like your product or not.

---

146   www.sharetribe.com/booklinks, #127

Net Promoter Score Survey

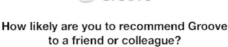

How likely are you to recommend Groove to a friend or colleague?

Not at all likely   Extremely likely

What is the most important reason for your score?

Submit Survey

NPS survey form by help desk company GrooveHQ

Responders are divided into three categories based on their answers:

- 9-10: Promoters. Promoters are loyal enthusiasts who will keep buying, and refers the service or the product to others.
- 7-8: Passives. Passives are not enthusiastic customers but they are satisfied with the product.
- 0-6: Detractors. Detractors are unhappy customers who will share their disappointment and affect your brand.

The score ranges from -100 (everybody is a detractor) to +100 (everybody is a promoter). It is calculated by subtracting the percentage of customers who are Detractors from the percentage of customers who are Promoters. An NPS that is positive (higher than zero) is considered good, and an NPS of +50 is excellent.

Remember to not pay too much attention to your initial rating since it is not very meaningful. Instead, you should follow the rating over time[147] to see if customer satisfaction is going up or down.

Do note that asking people about their willingness to recommend your marketplace is not always an accurate measure of user satisfaction. Juho and his team used NPS at Sharetribe and they noticed a surprising pattern: when contacting people who had given them a low score, quite a few replied by saying "I love your product, but it's my little secret, and I don't want to tell anyone else about it!" Thus, when you are conducting an NPS survey, be sure to also ask for the reasoning behind the rating.

To be fair, NPS has received quite a bit of criticism[148]. Among other things, some find it to be culturally insensitive and not as good a predictor as certain, more complex questionnaires. It is definitely not perfect but still a good starting point.

To minimize the effect of the issues mentioned above, using a second way of measuring user satisfaction is a good idea. We recommend the product/market fit survey.

The product/market fit survey

The product/market fit survey[149] was invented by Sean Ellis, founder and CEO of GrowthHackers.com. It is a very simple test that helps you understand whether you have achieved product/market fit.

In the product/market fit survey, you ask your users a simple question: "How would you feel if you could no longer use [product]?" There are four possible answers:

- Very disappointed

---

147   www.sharetribe.com/booklinks, #128
148   www.sharetribe.com/booklinks, #129
149   www.sharetribe.com/booklinks, #130

- Somewhat disappointed
- Not disappointed (it isn't really that useful)
- N/A – I no longer use [product]

Ellis compared the results from hundreds of companies. He figured out that if 40% of your users say they would be "very disappointed", you have quite likely achieved product/market fit.

The test has both pros and cons[150], but the clear upside is that it is very easy to set up and is very focused on your users and their willingness to use your product. It also complements NPS nicely since it focuses more directly on the value people are getting out of your product themselves instead of their willingness to recommend it.

How to measure the success of your personal trainer marketplace

Now that you know the most important metrics to follow, it is time to learn how to use them in practice. We will again focus on building a personal trainer marketplace, the example we have used in previous chapters.

First of all, you need to set up a system to collect data. For usage metrics, you set up Google Analytics. It is a great starting point since it is free and very flexible. It is very easy to set up and provides you with all usage metrics out of the box.

For transaction metrics and business metrics, no such standard tool exists. Instead, you simply build a spreadsheet and update the data manually every day. This approach does not scale to tens of thousands of users, but in the early days, it is a great, lean way to get started quickly.

Boris Wertz and Angela Tran Kingyans, the authors of the *Version One Marketplace Guide*[151], have put together a Marketplace KPI Spreadsheet[152]

---

150   www.sharetribe.com/booklinks, #131
151   www.sharetribe.com/booklinks, #21
152   www.sharetribe.com/booklinks, #132

which you use as a baseline. You also check out a similar spreadsheet[153] created by another venture capital firm, *daphni*. For visualizing the spreadsheet data, you get inspiration from the dashboards[154] put together by Vijay Nagappan of MHS Capital and use Keen.io and Plot.ly to build a dashboard.

You use Google Analytics to measure your customer conversion funnel. You dismissed a few paid alternatives (Mixpanel and Kissmetrics) that specialize in funnel tracking; while they were great to use, they are rather expensive and didn't fit your tight budget.

To measure NPS, you set up a free survey using UserReport's free tool[155]. You also set up the product/market fit test with the free Survey.io. Down the line, you might consider solid paid options for more advanced surveys and customer insights using UserVoice, Qualaroo, Typeform or SurveyMonkey.

After all this is set up, the data starts flowing in. You monitor the data weekly, and whenever you notice a suspicious pattern, you take appropriate action to correct the situation.

Summary

In this chapter, you have learned what the key performance indicators for marketplace businesses are. You should follow usage metrics, transaction metrics, business metrics, the customer conversion funnel, and user satisfaction metrics.

Usage metrics help you understand how many people visit your site and how they spend time there. The three most important figures are number of monthly visitors, bounce rate and time spent on site.

Transaction metrics help you understand whether your marketplace mechanics are working. The three most important metrics are liquidity, provider-to-customer ratio, and repeat purchase ratio.

---

153   www.sharetribe.com/booklinks, #133
154   www.sharetribe.com/booklinks, #134
155   www.sharetribe.com/booklinks, #135

Business metrics tell you how you are doing financially, and whether your business model is actually working. The three important KPIs are gross merchandise value, customer acquisition cost, and customer lifetime value.

Tracking the customer conversion funnel helps you understand where the biggest bottlenecks that prevent transactions from happening are. Starting from landing on your site, the funnel consists of the steps that a customer needs to take in order to complete a transaction.

All the previous figures tell you what is happening in your marketplace, but you also need to understand why. For that, you need to talk to your users. User satisfaction metrics help you put user feedback data in a quantifiable form. The two most important ones are Net Promoter Score and the product/market fit survey.

15

How to build trust in your marketplace

In the previous chapter, you learned how to measure the success of your marketplace. In this chapter, we will take a closer look at one of the most crucial components of a sustainable marketplace business: trust.

One of the biggest problems marketplace businesses need to tackle is fear. A 2015 PwC report noted that, among those who had participated in the sharing economy in the US, 57% said: "I am intrigued by companies in the sharing economy but have some concerns about them."[156]

Whenever customers and providers engage in transactions, multiple sources of anxiety emerge. What if I make a payment, but the provider never delivers the product? What if I rent my surfboard to a stranger and they break it by accident? What if this website leaks my credit card details to hackers? If these fears are not tackled in some way, they will prevent transactions from happening—no matter how big the customer need.

To address these fears, you need to build trust into your system. Your users need to trust your platform and each other. In this chapter, we will go through the most common ways to build trust in a marketplace community.

---

156   www.sharetribe.com/booklinks, #136

Understand the perceived risks

To understand what type of trust mechanisms you need, you first need to understand the type and size of your users' perceived risks. These risks can be both real or imaginary.

The amount of perceived risk varies widely depending on the type of the marketplace. Daan Weddepohl, co-founder of neighborhood sharing marketplace Peerby, liked to say that trust is overrated[157]. His users were able to trust each other without the need for any specific trust or safety mechanisms.

However, the reason this was possible is that the perceived risk for Peerby users was likely minimal. Peerby's user base was still relatively modest, which meant they were not an interesting target for scammers. Peerby mainly dealt in lending low-value items (like power drills) for free. There was no monetary transaction involved, which already helped—people are always warier when they need to spend money. The worst thing that could happen is that someone breaks your drill and refuses to pay for it; but even then, the loss is minimal. Peerby started their operations from Amsterdam, which is a relatively safe city, and their early adopter users were young "hipsters" who, in general, were eager to trust their peers.

To summarize, Peerby's example was not really one of not needing trust between its users, but having a situation where the level of trust was already high enough given their particular early adopter user segment and marketplace vertical. From this example, we can gather the most common things that affect the size of the perceived risk.

1. How many users do you have? As Boris Wertz and Angela Tran Kingyens note in their marketplace handbook, the need for trust-building typically grows with the size of your marketplace. Bigger platforms are more likely to attract bad actors.

2. What is the worst-case scenario? What is the worst thing that can happen? Losing 15 minutes of your life because you got stood up by

---

157   www.sharetribe.com/booklinks, #137

a random person from a Facebook flea market is not a big problem. Hiring an incompetent caretaker, which may result in harm to a loved one, is.

3. How much money is involved in an average transaction? This is related to the previous point. If you buy a used t-shirt online and never receive it, the situation is annoying, but not as bad as if you buy a used car that you never receive.

4. How trusting are your target users? Demographic and cultural factors can play a large role in this. The Sharetribe founders learned this first-hand when they launched a campus sharing marketplace in Finland and then tried to do the same in Chile. In the former, the response was excited and free of trust issues. In the latter, people responded with: "Are you crazy? I can't trust my peers enough to share with them."

Now that we know which factors you should pay attention to, we can start investigating the different tools marketplaces use to build trust.

Build trust between your users

Building a marketplace's trust mechanism is a process of evolution. The mechanism that is needed in the early days is different from the one needed when you achieve scale. Ridesharing company BlaBlaCar has gone through this process and studied the topic extensively. In cooperation with sharing economy researcher Arun Sundarajan, they even published a small e-book on the topic of trust[158]. In this section, we are going to introduce the different phases for building trust, moving from the early days to trust at scale.

Code of conduct – Create rules

The first thing you want to do is establish a set of rules on how things work on your platform. This is quite easy, and something we recommend having in place from the very beginning.

---

158   www.sharetribe.com/booklinks, #138

For instance, BlaBlaCar created guides on how to be a good driver and how to be a good passenger. This sets the expectation level of the users: as a driver, I should take care of the comfort of my passengers, while as a passenger, I should not cancel at the last minute. If everybody plays by the same rules, transactions will happen smoothly. Airbnb has a similar standards document[159].

In some cases, a set of rules is all you need to create a basic level of trust. This is what happens in the many local trade groups on Facebook. Facebook does not offer any specific tools for building trust, so administrators of these groups often create an elaborate set of rules. You should not overdo the rules, though—in many of these groups, problems arise from rule sets being too complicated, which leads to people forgetting about them.

Declaration – Get users to talk about themselves

To build trust, one of the first things BlaBlaCar did was to put effort into convincing users to share information about themselves. As CEO and founder Frédéric Mazzella explains:

> – *Users like to see and read the info but they are not willing to tell a lot of things about themselves (bio, picture, preferences). It's not that they don't want to share their information but it's not their goal. Their goal is to travel safely but they don't see the point of saying who they are. You need to make them understand why it's important.[160]*

BlaBlaCar users are asked to use their real name and a photo with their face clearly visible. Every user has a profile page, where they are asked to describe who they are.

Some marketplaces take this even further: instead of a free text description, you are asked a set of questions you need to answer. This is a nice way to get

---

159   www.sharetribe.com/booklinks, #139
160   www.sharetribe.com/booklinks, #140

people to add more detailed information about themselves. The more details there are in your profile, the easier it is for others to trust you.

Communication – Help users talk to each other

When Cristóbal started using Wallapop—an app to buy and sell stuff with nearby people we introduced earlier in the book—he was surprised about the lack of a reputation system (a heavier trust mechanism that we're going to discuss later). How could he trust other users? Some days later, when he used the app to buy a bike for his kid, he realized the main element to foster trust between sellers and buyers was the chat system. After finding an item you want to buy, you chat with the seller to figure out if the item is what you are looking for, and agree on the price.

Not having a reputation system was not a problem for the early adopters— after chatting with the seller, buyers felt secure enough to meet them at a nearby location and buy the item. Since then, Wallapop has grown tremendously and nowadays has a reputation system, but just like with Peerby, the initial lack of such a system was not a barrier to entry.

People typically fear the unknown. If they do not know the other person at all, it increases fear. A simple way to help people trust each other is to offer them a low-key communication channel. This is why most peer-to-peer marketplaces offer their users an internal messaging system they can use to have a chat before actually engaging in a transaction.

Social dimension – Show users how they are connected

Like we noted earlier, people fear the unknown. But is the other person really a stranger? After all, according to the idea of "six degrees of separation"[161], we are all connected to each other. If you can make these connections visible, it makes it easier for people to trust each other.

---

161   www.sharetribe.com/booklinks, #141

Airbnb did this in a clever way by introducing social connections. By using data from Facebook, they allowed people to filter listings based on common friends with the host. You might travel to Paris and note that a friend of a friend has a flat there. While you do not know this person directly, you immediately trust them more because of our mutual connection. You know, at least, that they are a real person, and if you want further proof of their trustworthiness, you can ask your friend.

Verification – Improve the quality of users

If we do not share any mutual Facebook friends with another user, how can you know they are who they say they are, or even a real person? After all, "on the internet, nobody knows you're a dog"[162]. No absolutely foolproof methods for identity verification exist, but there are several things you can do to decrease the probability of fraud.

The most basic verification is email validation. Practically all websites that allow their users to create an account use this verification method. However, creating a fake email account that cannot be traced to any individual is easy, so this step is not enough.

The next most common step is phone number validation. Typically, this is done by sending an SMS with a code to the phone number provided by the user, which then needs to be entered into the service to verify that the user owns the number. eBay uses a system that automatically calls users' phone numbers to verify their identity. However, prepaid phone subscriptions are quite common, so this method is also not enough to reveal the identity of the user.

Verifying social network accounts is often useful, even without having mutual connections. Seeing that the other user has 200+ friends on Facebook means that it is likely not an entirely fake account.

---

162   www.sharetribe.com/booklinks, #142

How about verifying the exact home address of the user? This is what NextDoor, a social network and marketplace for neighborhoods, does. Part of their value proposition is that all the people in your neighborhood group are your actual neighbors, so it is important for them to make sure that is actually the case. They use a relatively complex process that includes, among other things, sending a postcard with a secret code to the user's home address[163]. The process is secure, but the downside is that it creates a lot of friction, and might prevent potential users from joining the site.

Such a complex process can sometimes be worth it. As we have learned in previous chapters, it is often a good idea to focus on quality over quantity. In the offline world, your identity is typically verified by showing an ID card or a passport. Today, this is also possible online thanks to advanced image recognition technology. Airbnb requires hosts to verify their identity by scanning their ID document and allows hosts to require their guests to have gone through the same process. Companies like Jumio allow marketplace entrepreneurs to automate the entire ID verification process.

Sometimes it is not enough to know that the person is real. You may want to know more about their background; perhaps they have a criminal record or a history of bad credit. For this, a background check is needed. Background checks are commonly used by labor marketplaces—specifically, ones where the type of the service requires you to allow a stranger into your home. In the early days of a marketplace, you can conduct background checks manually by calling or emailing each provider and asking them for information. When you scale, that is no longer possible. Companies like Checkr and Onfido allow you to automate the entire process through a convenient API.

Reputation – Punish bad behavior

Even with precautionary measures, something bad will eventually happen. It might not even be due to malicious reasons, but simply because

---

163   www.sharetribe.com/booklinks, #143

of carelessness: a seller forgets to ship the item they promised, or a customer scratches a rented car. Most marketplaces that scale also need to deal with an increasing amount of attempted fraud.

The traditional way for marketplaces to tackle these situations is by using a reputation system. This was pioneered by eBay, which popularized the practice of the buyer and the seller reviewing each other after a successful transaction. Each user's profile displays a "reputation score"—a summary of their reputation.

Each eBay user has a comprehensive feedback profile

Typically, a review consists of a numeric evaluation (a one to five-star rating, or a simple thumbs up or down) and a text section. This captures both the quantitative and the qualitative aspect of the review. In some cases, you might want to ask the parties to give a numeric rating for different aspects of the transaction. This is especially helpful in large marketplaces with lots of providers and reviews since it helps providers differentiate their offerings.

For example, Airbnb asks the guest to rate things like communication, cleanliness, and location separately, which all add up to the final rating. A guest might be friendly and timely but create a huge mess. An appropriate rating helps other hosts know what to expect without labeling the guest as a malicious actor.

Airbnb asks users to rate each other for several different criteria

eBay's system has been studied extensively[164], and researchers have found that sellers with higher reputation scores are able to charge higher prices for their products. Maintaining a good reputation is vital to them. Today, almost all popular marketplaces use similar reputation systems.

There's an additional benefit to using such systems: they discourage users from bypassing the marketplace's payment system.

Review data is often used to weed out bad apples. Uber and Lyft ask both drivers and passengers to rate their experience at the end of a ride. These companies remove poorly rated drivers (with an average of 3 stars or less) from the system, removing the need for passengers to read reviews before getting a ride. BlaBlaCar also uses a similar mechanism.

Juho noticed this after having a bad experience with a BlaBlaCar driver. Two weeks after the incident, Juho tried to leave a negative rating for the driver, but it was too late: the driver had already been removed from the platform due to negative ratings from others.

Although implementing a reputation system fosters trust, research shows that these systems rarely build sufficient trust or provide adequate safety on their own. As Andrei Hagiu and Simon Rothman note in Harvard Business Review:

– *Many online rating & review systems suffer from significant biases: People who voluntarily rate a product or service tend to be either very happy or very unhappy with it. This severely undermines the value of the information provided and skews results.[165]*

Besides bias, another problem with reputation is that even when it is transaction-based, you can still fake it. For instance, you could create several fake accounts, and have them conduct transactions with each other and leave positive reviews.

164   www.sharetribe.com/booklinks, #144
165   www.sharetribe.com/booklinks, #22

Feedback extortion is another common problem in popular marketplaces: "If you're going to give me a bad review, I'll give you one as well." Extortion can also be used to get additional value from the other party. Airbnb tackles extortion by using a "double blind" review system: both parties have 14 days to leave the review, after which both reviews are published simultaneously. Once the reviews are published, they can no longer be altered. If you use a two-sided reputation system in your marketplace, we highly recommend using a similar system. Airbnb also has an extortion policy[166] that specifically prohibits this type of behavior.

To summarize, while reputation systems play an essential role in creating trust between marketplace users, they should not be trusted blindly. They offer one data point that should be complemented with other mechanisms.

Build trust in your platform

Not all of your users' fears are related to the person they are transacting with. They also need to trust your platform with their money and information. This challenge is particularly big for new marketplace businesses—ones without a proven brand and track record.

Sharing economy expert Rachel Botsman, the author of the excellent book *Who Can You Trust167*, talks about a concept called the trust stack[168]. It describes three layers in which trust is created. First, the person needs to trust an idea—it would be feasible to rent my car to a stranger, for instance. Second, the person needs to trust the platform. Only once these two things are established, you can take the third step of trusting a particular stranger on the platform.

We will now review the most common strategies to make your platform appear more trustworthy in the eyes of your users.

---

166   www.sharetribe.com/booklinks, #145
167   www.sharetribe.com/booklinks, #146
168   www.sharetribe.com/booklinks, #147

A good first impression

We will never forget the experience of using Airbnb for the first time. It had the most unique, beautiful, and functional design of all the marketplaces we knew at the time. The user experience was stunning. This was no accident: founders Brian Chesky and Joe Gebbia were both designers. From the beginning, they had designed for trust. As Gebbia notes in his TED talk:

> – *We bet our whole company on the hope that, with the right design, people will be willing to overcome the stranger-danger bias.*[169]

Anand Iyer, CEO & Founder of Trusted and previous CPO of Threadflip, explains that a first impression is a key mechanism in fostering trust:

> – *By baking trustworthiness into users' very first touch point with your product, you not only build a solid relationship between them and your brand, but with each other as they exchange goods and services.*[170]

One facet of design that helps build trust is polishing the small details. Make sure that the grammar of your copy is correct, and that your visuals look professional. Nothing screams "scam" more loudly than a quickly built platform with bad copy, obvious stock photos, and awkward design choices.

A great way to build trust is to use social proof on your landing page. BlaBlaCar does this by highlighting positive user testimonials near the top of the page. To learn more about building a good first impression, reread chapter eight on communicating your value proposition.

Content curation

As we have mentioned multiple times in previous chapters of this book, it is important to focus on quality over quantity, especially during the early days of your marketplace. Be exclusive and hand-pick only the best providers, products, and services.

---

169   www.sharetribe.com/booklinks, #148
170   www.sharetribe.com/booklinks, #149

Joel Serra, former head of launch at EatWith, a marketplace for home-cooked dinner events, explains how for the first year and a half, EatWith manually curated every event[171]. They knew the attendees and the mix of gender, age, and languages for each event. It was not scalable, but because of this approach, they were able to ensure a great experience for their early users and build their reputation as a trustworthy platform.

One way to invest in the quality of the initial content is to eat your own dog food and purchase regularly from your own providers. The founders of Airbnb did exactly this in their early days. Brian Chesky even gave up his apartment and lived entirely off of Airbnb for a while. By doing this, he came to understand the little details that make or break the customer experience, and Airbnb was able to instruct the hosts to pay attention to them.

Deliver what you promise

When you are crafting your value proposition, be extremely mindful of only promising things you know you can keep. If you fail to deliver on your promise, your reputation and trustworthiness will suffer.

Airbnb experienced this first-hand when a guest ransacked an Airbnb host's apartment[172] in 2011. The host wrote a long blog post about the incident, detailing how Airbnb had betrayed her specifically because it promised that the site and its users can be trusted. This was in stark contrast to Craigslist, a site she had previously used, which specifically advised users to use it at their own risk. The blog post and the hype that followed caused lots of trouble for Airbnb—trouble it could have avoided by being clearer in its communication.

Many labor marketplaces like Uber and TaskRabbit guarantee a high service level. This also means they need to act on that promise. Oisin Hanrahan, CEO of labor marketplace Handy, says that if their providers do not show up on time, the customers' trust in the platform is shattered.[173]

---

171   www.sharetribe.com/booklinks, #150
172   www.sharetribe.com/booklinks, #151
173   www.sharetribe.com/booklinks, #116

Address issues quickly and transparently

When Airbnb was hit with the ransacking issue, they reacted quickly. Brian Chesky wrote a post[174] explaining all the actions they immediately took to ensure such a case would never happen again. Airbnb's customer service team was alert, and the host whose place was ransacked made a point to stress that their level of support had been great. This reaction helped Airbnb survive the crisis.

Eventually, something will go wrong. You cannot prevent all negative events, but you can mitigate the damage by reacting to them in a fast and transparent way. Apologize. Tell the customer you really screwed up, and will do you everything in your power to make sure it will not happen again—preferably stating what concrete changes you plan on making, and then following through with them. Refund the customer or provider who experienced the problem, and maybe even provide them with extra credits.

When the shit hits the fan, you might actually end up better off than when you started: providing a great customer (or provider) experience in such a situation can completely turn a bad situation around and actually improve the reputation of your platform.

Reduce the risk

It is good to keep in mind that your users do not always need to really trust each other. It might be enough if they can trust the experience: if they partake in a transaction, nothing too bad will happen, even if the other party is unreliable. In this section, we are going to take a look at ways to reduce the perceived risk without actually building trust.

Frictionless payments, escrow, insurance and deposits

Guaranteeing a smooth and trustworthy transaction process and covering for situations where something goes wrong is a great way to reduce user risk.

---

174   www.sharetribe.com/booklinks, #152

This can be the most important value proposition of a marketplace business, and a great way to prevent disintermediation.

The best way to do this is to provide a frictionless and secure payment system. It can be coupled with things like insurance, refundable deposits, guarantees, or buyer and seller protection.

We spent a lot of time with this particular topic in chapter four in which we discussed the different ways a marketplace business can provide value to its users. We won't repeat the details of these mechanisms here, so check out the chapter if you haven't already done so.

The blockchain and "trustless trust"

An interesting technological development that might affect the way marketplace transactions happen in the future is the emergence of the blockchain, a distributed, trusted database that already powers plenty of applications. The most well-known of them is the digital currency Bitcoin. Bitcoin allows people to transact with each other online in a secure way without the help of intermediaries such as banks or credit card companies.

As LinkedIn founder and prominent investor Reid Hoffman writes:

– *The blockchain creates the possibility of trustless trust. Parties no longer need to know or trust each other to participate in exchanges of value with absolute assurance and no intermediaries.*[175]

The distributed nature of the blockchain and cryptocurrency payments remove issues related to credit card fraud and other types of fraudulent transactions. This means you do not need to trust the other party at all because you know that a transaction with them will happen without a hitch.

Blockchain development is still in its infancy, and it is not yet very practical for layman use. However, we do expect the development to be fast in the

---

175   www.sharetribe.com/booklinks, #153

coming years. If you want to learn more about how blockchain can be applied to marketplaces, we encourage you to take a look at the OpenBazaar project[176].

How to build trust for your personal trainer marketplace

Now that you have learned ways to foster trust and safety, it is time to put them into practice. We will again focus on building a personal trainer marketplace, the imaginary example marketplace from previous chapters.

You start off by defining clear rules for both customers and trainers. You write a cancellation policy, instructions on what to do if the level of service is not adequate, and a guide on how to offer great customer service as a trainer. You tweak a few pages on your marketplace to ensure every user will read these guidelines.

To ensure high-quality supply, you only accept trainers who have an official personal training license as your providers. You manually vet each provider and ask them to submit this information. You also tell your customers that every provider has been vetted and hand-picked.

You allow each user (both customers and providers) to create their own profile page where they can add their name, photo, and a description of themselves. You encourage everyone to use their real name. You also allow providers to add videos to describe their services. This helps build an even better connection between them and their potential customers before a transaction. You check each profile to make sure all the details are in order and even check the text for grammatical errors.

You decide to add a messaging system to your site, allowing customers and providers to contact each other and exchange information before a transaction. This helps build a connection between them.

You also add a simple reputation system where both parties can rate each other. As your marketplace scales, you will allow the customers to rate several different aspects of each transaction: Was the trainer friendly? Did they know

---

176   https://openbazaar.org/

what they were doing? Did they arrive on time? If your providers constantly get bad reviews, you remove them from the platform.

To avoid last-minute cancellations, you offer a booking process where the customer can find the desired time slot and make the payment immediately. Since you have established a clear cancellation policy, customers who cancel at the last minute will not get their money back.

To protect customers, you offer a buyer protection program by using PayPal as your payment provider. You guarantee that if a provider is a no-show or provides bad service, the customer will get their money back. Eventually, when you scale, you plan on adding an insurance program that covers the medical treatment of customers who hurt themselves because of improper instructions from their trainers.

Summary

In this chapter, you learned why building trust is vital in order to grow your marketplace business. You need to build trust between your customers and providers, and also help your users trust the platform itself. You are aware of methods to reduce the perceived risk of a marketplace without having to build trust.

The most important ways to build trust between your users are by creating rules, encouraging users to tell more about themselves, providing a messaging system between users, showing users how they are connected to each other, verifying their identities and backgrounds, and by using a reputation system.

To encourage your users to trust your platform, you should offer a good first impression, curate your content, deliver what you promise, and address issues quickly and transparently.

You can reduce the perceived risks of your marketplace with frictionless online payments, insurance and other provider protection measures, escrow, and other customer protection measures. In the future, blockchain technology can play a big part in creating "trustless trust".

Now that you have a growing base of users who trust each other, you are all set to scale.

16

How to turn your marketplace into a community

In the previous chapter, you learned how to build trust in your marketplace. In this final chapter, we will take a closer look at a strategy marketplaces use to create a sustainable competitive advantage: community-building.

We've repeated this over and over again, but let's state it one more time: the purpose of any marketplace is to facilitate transactions between users. To do that, you need to have users who are engaged and committed to your platform. A popular way to achieve this is to turn your platform something more than a marketplace: a community. This strategy has been used by the most popular marketplaces such as Airbnb and Etsy. You will now learn how to do the same.

Why you should build a community

Before we dive deeper into the strategies for building communities, we need to ask "Why?". What are the tangible benefits that an engaged community of users can provide a marketplace business?

Let's start by defining what we mean by the word "community" in the context of a marketplace. Wikipedia defines community as a group of people who share something in common, such as norms, values or identity. Essentially, building a community around your marketplace means making your users feel that the marketplace is a part of their identity.

An Airbnb user is a person who allows strangers into their home and stays in strangers' homes when traveling. An Etsy seller is a person who makes a living as a maker and quite likely buys what she needs from other makers. These behaviors are an essential part of their identities.

There are several reasons why it is important to get people to identify with your marketplace. Let's go through them.

Engaged users buy more

As you learned in chapter 14 on marketplace metrics, getting a new customer requires a lot more work than engaging an old one. You should aim for a high repeat purchase ratio, thus increasing customer lifetime value. If your users feel the marketplace is part of their identity, they will keep coming back, and they will buy more.

Etsy is a great example of this. Etsy defines itself as follows: "We're more than a marketplace: we're a community of artists, creators, collectors, thinkers and doers." Their emphasis on the community is quite likely a key reason why their customers keep coming back; in 2015, 81% of Etsy's sales came from repeat purchases[177].

Engaged users are loyal. When they feel they belong to a community, they are less likely to jump ship, even when a competitor tries to entice them with lower prices or other perks.

Engaged users trust each other

As was brought up in the previous chapter, a lack of trust between customers and providers is a big challenge for many marketplaces. If your users feel they share the same values and norms, it will increase the trust between them. And if they trust each other more, they will engage in transactions with each other more often.

---

177   www.sharetribe.com/booklinks, #155

Building trust through a community has been important for EatWith, an "Airbnb for home cooked meals". This is how Joel Serra, EatWith's former head of launch, describes the early days of the company:

– *We could have easily had ten or twenty thousand chefs in a few months because there were so many people looking to become chefs. However, we decided to grow slowly and get to know our community on a personal basis. We wanted to have a really personal relationship with everyone in our community to create the basic level of trust. Knowing every host around the world, whether it's through a conversation over Skype or through going to their event, creates the level of trust that a lot of platforms in this space simply don't have.[178]*

Engaged users help you grow

In chapter 13, while discussing different growth strategies for marketplaces, we mentioned that community building is an important source of growth. You want to reach a virtuous cycle where high-quality providers bring in more customers and vice versa.

As Rachel Botsman writes:

– *"How does it make you feel?" is a question I commonly ask when I meet hosts on Airbnb, drivers on Lyft or Taskrunners on Taskrabbit to try to understand the role this rising breed of companies in the collaborative economy plays in people's lives. What I have noticed is that I often don't get a simple answer but they tell me a story, their story of why they are doing what they are doing. And embedded in these tales is a cult-like sentiment that could rival Apple devotees, Harley Davidson fanatics or Star Trek groupies.[179]*

---

178   www.sharetribe.com/booklinks, #150
179   www.sharetribe.com/booklinks, #156

These three successful companies have spent very little on traditional advertising and have relatively small marketing teams compared to established brands. Instead, they spend lots of resources on community-building. As a result, they have turned their most engaged users into ambassadors, who constantly spread the positive word about their brand.

Engaged users help you improve your platform

Building a marketplace business is a continuous learning process. You should launch your platform as early as possible since you only start learning once you put something in front of your users.

Feedback from your users plays a crucial part in understanding their biggest needs. If your users are more engaged, they care more about your product, which also means they will give more feedback. When something is not working, they will complain about it right away, very vocally. This is great. When people give you angry feedback, it's a sign that they care.

This feedback is, by far, the best way to help prioritize what to work on next. If you are not getting any feedback, it likely means you are not solving a problem for your users and they are not engaged. It is an indicator that something needs to be changed, drastically.

How to build a community

As you can see, building a community has plenty of benefits. So how do you actually go about doing it?

Since marketplaces are two-sided beasts, you first want to understand which side to focus on. In some cases, it might make sense to involve all your users in the same community, especially if they act as both a customer and a provider. This is the approach ridesharing marketplace BlaBlaCar took: they highlight stories of both drivers and passengers on the same page[180].

---

180   www.sharetribe.com/booklinks, #157

The current trend, however, seems to be to focus on a marketplace's most valuable user group: the providers. For instance, Airbnb's community center[181] is clearly targeted at hosts, even though some of their meetups are open to guests as well. Etsy, Uber, and Thumbtack use a similar strategy, focusing their community efforts on sellers, drivers, and pros, respectively.

Airbnb mainly targets hosts with its community area

As your platform grows, you might even consider building several communities. Etsy has so many providers that it's increasingly difficult to create a feeling of belonging to a global community. Their solution has been to build "teams" that focus on specific areas of interest[182]. For instance, The Old Farmhouse Gathering is a group that appeals primarily to whimsical and folk art crafters.

---

181   www.sharetribe.com/booklinks, #158
182   www.sharetribe.com/booklinks, #159

There are several different approaches for building a community. What works best for you depends on the stage and type of your marketplace. We will now review the most common strategies.

Define your mission

The first step in building a community is to think about what you stand for[183]. What is the purpose of your marketplace business? What change do you want to see in the world? If you want your users to identify with your marketplace, they need to identify with this mission. Our recommendation is to think about your mission from the very beginning, way before you launch your platform or even start talking to your users. Clarifying your mission—both internally and externally—will help you identify the people who relate to that mission.

Airbnb has put a lot of effort into understanding their essence. As Airbnb founder and CEO Brian Chesky puts it:

> – *For so long, people thought Airbnb was about renting houses. But really, we're about home. You see, a house is just a space, but a home is where you belong. And what makes this global community so special is that for the very first time, you can belong anywhere. That is the idea at the core of our company: belonging.[184]*

This is an idea that resonates with many travelers: your home is where you lay your hat.

Etsy, meanwhile, stands for handmade items. In 2007, Etsy—along with partners—released a Buy Handmade manifesto[185], and urged people to pledge to buy more handmade since it is better for the people and the planet. Naturally, this is a message that resonates with crafters.

Remember: when you stand for something, it usually means you also stand against something else. Airbnb stands against impersonal hotel experiences.

---

183 www.sharetribe.com/booklinks, #160
184 www.sharetribe.com/booklinks, #161
185 www.sharetribe.com/booklinks, #162

Etsy has traditionally stood against mass production. Do not try to have a mission that resonates with everyone. The result will be a bland statement that nobody really identifies with. Instead, be bold, and be prepared to make some enemies along the way.

Once you have clarified your mission, you need to stay true to it or you will be alienating your community. Etsy recently embraced mass production[186] to reap more profits. The move caused many original sellers to abandon the site[187], and damaged Etsy's reputation.

Tap into existing communities

Instead of building a community from scratch, see if a community already exists around your cause. As Facebook founder Mark Zuckerberg said when he was asked about how to build an online community:

> – *Communities already exist. Instead, think about how you can help that community do what it wants to do.*[188]

Etsy was born out of a need of an existing community. As one of the co-founders, Chris Maguire, explains, the founders were running a freelance web design shop before Etsy. One of their projects was a redesign of an online forum for crafters, GetCrafty. The founders became active members of the forum and soon realized many of the forum members wanted a place to sell their creations online. They went on to build such a solution. While building it they discovered an even bigger forum, Craftster.org. They contacted the founder and suddenly had a huge audience.[189]

Know your early members

While you want to think about your mission before you have any users, it is good to keep in mind that ultimately it is the users, not you, who define

---

186   www.sharetribe.com/booklinks, #163
187   www.sharetribe.com/booklinks, #164
188   www.sharetribe.com/booklinks, #165
189   www.sharetribe.com/booklinks, #166

your community. Thus, it is important to get to know them early own—to understand their needs, and learn how to talk to them.

Brian Chesky was homeless for months[190], living with one Airbnb host to another. He wanted to know everything about the service and its users. He received important feedback and built relationships with their early adopters.

The EatWith team hosted dinners themselves or participated as attendees in other dinners. They did this to get to meet the customers in real life, better understand the EatWith experience, and keep learning about their service.

Allow people to interact with each other

Once you have found the people that identify with your mission, you need to help them communicate with each other. You should offer some kind of communication platform that lets people interact freely without the need to engage in a transaction. This helps them realize that instead of being alone, they are surrounded by like-minded individuals who identify with the same mission.

Most popular marketplaces—like Airbnb, eBay, Etsy, and Uber—offer community forums where their users can interact with each other. Starting with a more lightweight approach can be enough; perhaps a Facebook group, or even just a hashtag on Twitter or Instagram.

Facilitate conversations

During your forum's early days, you will face the same problem as with your marketplace: it is empty and needs a critical mass of users to function properly. Just like you need to seed your marketplace, you also need to seed your online community[191].

One way to seed content is to start discussion threads yourself. A great way to get people to talk is by asking them questions. People love to talk about themselves. Create an introduction thread where every new provider can

---

190   www.sharetribe.com/booklinks, #167
191   www.sharetribe.com/booklinks, #168

tell a bit about themselves and why they joined. This not only helps seed the community but also helps people trust each other as they hear each others' stories and realize there's another human being behind that avatar.

Seeding also helps set the tone of the community. Others will follow the example of the early adopters. When popular online community site Reddit got started, its founders went quite far with this strategy: they created fake accounts[192] and had conversations with each other just to showcase what a civilized conversation on Reddit could look like.

When your users start creating their own threads on the forum, make sure every thread gets a response. People want their voice to be heard.

Highlight your users' stories

When new people join your community, they want to learn what the community is like. Sharing the stories of your users helps them familiarize themselves with existing members. BlaBlaCar, for example, invests heavily in showcasing users stories on their BlaBlaStories site. Thumbtack also highlights stories from their successful professionals and happy customers.

---

192   www.sharetribe.com/booklinks, #169

BLABLASTARS

Meet our BlaBlaStar, David!

MORE STORIES ABOUT BLABLASTORIES ↓

| BLABLASTARS | BLABLASTARS | VIGNETTES | BLABLASTARS |
| Meet our BlaBlaStar, Marshell! | Meet Maria! | Guest Blog Post: My First BlaBlaCar Experience! | Meet our BlaBlaStar, Diana |

BlaBlaCar highlights the stories of its users

Obviously, these stories communicate the benefits of the marketplace, but they also have another purpose: by reading a few stories, you get a basic understanding of the kind of people who belong to the community. More importantly, you can also decide whether they are the kind of people you would feel comfortable hanging out with.

Celebrate power users

When your marketplace grows, you will notice certain users who bring in a lot more sales than everyone else. These people are your power users. Consider offering them special perks and advantages.

Airbnb has a SuperHost program[193] that rewards hosts who offer excellent customer experiences. SuperHosts receive travel coupons, priority support,

---

193   www.sharetribe.com/booklinks, #170

and other similar perks. Ebay has a PowerSeller program[194] that rewards qualified sellers for reaching specific goals around sales volume, feedback, policy compliance, and account standing.

Curate the community

Similarly to how you want to highlight certain members of the community, you also want to weed out the bad apples and remove inappropriate content. In active forums, moderation can be quite a time-consuming task as you need to go over a large amount of content every day. This means you should only open a forum once you know you have enough time to maintain and curate it.

According to Nish Nadaraja, the creator of review site Yelp's Elite program, when building a community, one of the first things to figure out is a mechanism for conflict resolution[195]. Conflicts are inevitable. It is a good idea to set clear ground rules and provide an example by being active in the community yourself.

Note: do not confuse moderation with censorship. While you want to remove users that are aggressive or malicious towards other users, you should not remove users or content that criticizes your platform or customer service. Doing this will backfire. This type of action will not go unnoticed and users will interpret it as an attempt to silence valid criticism. A better way to respond is by addressing the critique politely but firmly, and explaining your position.

Go to the streets

In some cases, it is not enough to build the community online. Interacting with people in real life can be a much more effective method to engage them. Rebecca Rosenfelt, Product Manager at Airbnb Portland, explains how Airbnb uses guerrilla tactics whenever they need to build a community in new regions. They build teams of two or three people and send them to talk to locals, host info sessions, distribute flyers, and set up booths at local events. She says the CAC

---

194   www.sharetribe.com/booklinks, #171
195   www.sharetribe.com/booklinks, #160

(Customer Acquisition Cost) for this strategy (physical presence) is one-fifth the cost as with Facebook ads. Additionally, the markets where Airbnb had a physical presence kept growing twice as fast as their other markets.[196]

Lyft created the role of ambassador[197] to give users the opportunity to promote Lyft in their city in exchange for cash. Ambassadors can earn $10 per passenger referral, and up to $750 for each referred driver.

Host local events

When your community grows, you can move from piggybacking on others' events to hosting your own. Local events are a great way to get a big group of your users to the same physical location at the same time. The people who attend such events are likely potential power users.

Airbnb organizes meetups to help hosts (and guests) meet each other and learn about topics related to the service. Airbnb also organizes launch parties whenever they open in new countries and cities. BlaBlaCar hosts BlaBlaCar drinks and BlaBlaCar tours around differents regions to raise awareness about the brand and build a community.

When EatWith launched in Barcelona, Cristóbal (together with others in the OuiShare[198] Barcelona team) helped them organize a "fighting tapas" event with eight of their hosts. The event was a great success, and more than 120 people attended.

How to turn your personal trainer marketplace into a community

As we have done in previous chapters, it is time to apply—one last time—the learnings from this chapter to your imaginary personal trainer marketplace.

You start by defining your mission. Since your marketplace deals with health and fitness, you decide to go with "fitness is for everyone". You reason

196   www.sharetribe.com/booklinks, #87
197   www.sharetribe.com/booklinks, #172
198   http://ouishare.net/

that when the barrier to start exercising is low enough, more people will start exercising, which results in improved overall health and life expectancy. This resonates with people who are interested in getting healthier but have so far been unable to get off the couch. It also resonates with your trainers since it promises more customers for them.

Since your customers and providers are two separate groups—personal trainers rarely use the services of other personal trainers—you decide to focus your community-building efforts on your most valuable users: the trainers. Being a freelance personal trainer is often a lonely job, so you figure they could benefit immensely from being a part of a trainer community.

In chapter eleven on building supply, you had decided to get your early adopter providers by tapping into existing communities: local gyms. You decide to book personal training sessions yourself with your 50 first providers, simply to get to know them and learn how they operate.

You then set up an invite-only Facebook group and invite all your providers. You make the group secret to create a feeling of exclusivity. In the group, you ask each trainer to introduce themselves and ask them to share their best customer service tips. You continue initiating discussions in the group about topics that interest the trainers, and create polls to let them easily share their opinions.

In your blog, you start highlighting the stories of your top providers. You interview them and create long, detailed articles about their backgrounds and why they are doing what they do. You also feature the best of these articles on the landing page of your marketplace. You also start a local meetup group to let the trainers meet each other and exchange tips in person. When you launch in new cities, you set up similar groups in each city.

As your marketplace grows, you create a "trainer hero" program to celebrate trainers with the most bookings and best reviews. You offer them fee discounts and throw exclusive parties only for them.

Summary

In this final chapter, you have learned why it is beneficial to turn your marketplace into a community. Engaged community members buy more, trust each other more, help you grow by spreading the word, and provide valuable feedback that helps you improve your offering.

To build a community, you should start by defining your mission: what do you stand for? You then need to decide whether to focus your community-building efforts on all of your users, or focus only on your customers or providers.

Community-building strategies include tapping into existing communities, getting to know your early members, allowing people to communicate with each other, facilitating conversations, highlighting the stories of your users, celebrating power users, curating the community, creating street teams, and participating in and organizing local events.

Final thoughts

On these pages, we've taken you through a journey to the world of marketplace businesses. You've learned how to validate your concept, build your platform, grow your user base, and, most importantly, facilitate transactions between your users. We've painted a big picture and also dived in the nitty-gritty details.

If this book helps you avoid just one out of the numerous mistakes we've made ourselves when building online marketplaces over the past ten years, we consider it a huge success.

But there's only so much you can learn from a book. The best way to learn—by far—is to get out of the building and start building your own marketplace business. Every such business has its own unique challenges. We guarantee that you'll get to make plenty of mistakes and fail many times over. What he hope you've gotten out of this book is the ability to fail fast, learn from your experiences, and quickly change your course.

Building a marketplace business is extremely challenging, but also very rewarding. Whatever happens to your business, you can be sure that you will not regret choosing this path. If nothing else, it will bring you the adventure of a lifetime.

Good luck, entrepreneur!

In Helsinki and Barcelona in February 2018,
Juho Makkonen and Cristóbal Gracia

Enjoyed the book?

Please leave a review on Amazon: www.sharetribe.com/amazon-review

It will help us enormously.

Enjoyed the links?

Email us at book@sharetribe.com with subject line "Links PDF" to receive a handy PDF with all the links to the articles that the book refers to.

About the authors

Juho Makkonen has been building online marketplaces since 2008. In 2011, he co-founded Sharetribe, a company that helps people and organizations to create their own online marketplace platforms and build successful businesses around them. He currently serves as the CEO of the company. Juho is a long time advocate of the sharing economy whose writings have appeared in Shareable Magazine and OuiShare Magazine, among others. He lives in Helsinki with his wife and dog.

Cristóbal Gracia built his first peer-to-peer marketplace in 2009. Today, he is a member of the Platform Design Toolkit team, works as an advisor for marketplace startups, and facilitates lectures, talks and workshops. He is also a member of the global collaborative economy network OuiShare. He lives between Hungary and Spain with his wife and two children.

Thanks for reading.

Find more on www.sharetribe.com/academy